PRAISE FOR *LIFT US UP, DON'T PUSH US OUT!*

"*Lift Us Up, Don't Push Us Out!* is a bold and exciting book that presents the stories we never hear—powerful stories of successful grassroots organizing in schools and communities across the nation led by parents, students, educators, and allies. The lessons we can learn from these inspiring activists and campaigns need to be spread far and wide. They show how social justice unionism plays a vital role in the fight for equity and justice for all our children and in the growing movement against privatization of public education."

—KAREN LEWIS, president of the Chicago Teachers Union

"Full of powerful ideas, powerful examples, powerful policy strategies, and powerful people, this book touches both mind and heart. These compelling stories—told by those who lived them—teach us about and advance the much-needed educational justice movement."

—JEANNIE OAKES, Presidential Professor Emeritus,
University of California at Los Angeles, and author of
Keeping Track: How Schools Structure Inequality

"Each one of the essays is a tour de force. You are captivated by the passion, the fury, the courage, the honesty, and the determination that is expressed so brilliantly by the writers, who have found a way, by working arm-in-arm with others, to fight for educational justice for *all* children. This book brings the powerful and authentic voices of parent and community movement leaders into our classrooms and communities."

—KAREN MAPP, senior lecturer on education,
Harvard Graduate School of Education

"Featuring diverse and powerful stories of fights against the corporate degradation of American schooling, *Lift Us Up, Don't Push Us Out!* weaves an inspiring vision of what education could and should be if we valued all children and their potential. It could hardly be more timely."

—CHARLES PAYNE, author of *So Much Reform,
So Little Change: The Persistence of Failure in Urban Schools*

"At last! This book of victorious stories guides us through the resistance to racism and assaults on public schools. It is incredibly inspiring to see how educators, students, parents, and community organizations—people of color, in particular—are joining in the fight back to defeat school closures, charter expansions, and other privatization schemes. Organizing is key as uplifting policy solutions, community schools, and intergenerational movement-building replace appalling alienation and rampant disinvestment in education."

—DR. JOYCE E. KING, Benjamin E. Mays Endowed Chair for
Urban Teaching, Learning, and Leadership, Georgia State University

"*Lift Us Up, Don't Push Us Out!* weaves together the stories of parent organizers, student activists, and committed educators who are forging a powerful movement for educational justice across the United States. Through compelling first-person narratives, the book highlights grassroots activism as a strategy for making schools culturally responsive, inclusive, and equitable."

—JOHN ROGERS, professor of education,
University of California at Los Angeles, and director of
UCLA's Institute for Democracy, Education, and Access (IDEA)

LIFT US UP, DON'T PUSH US OUT!

LIFT US UP,

DON'T PUSH US OUT!

VOICES FROM THE FRONT LINES
OF THE EDUCATIONAL JUSTICE MOVEMENT

MARK R. WARREN
WITH DAVID GOODMAN

BEACON PRESS, BOSTON

Beacon Press
Boston, Massachusetts
www.beacon.org

Beacon Press books
are published under the auspices of
the Unitarian Universalist Association of Congregations.

21 20 19 18   8 7 6 5 4 3 2 1

This book is printed on acid-free paper that meets the uncoated paper
ANSI/NISO specifications for permanence as revised in 1992.

Text design and composition by Kim Arney

Cover graphic: The Lift Us Up, Don't Push Us Out! slogan and graphic were designed
by Brian Butler and commissioned and adopted by the Dignity in Schools Campaign
for its 2016 Week of Action Against School Pushout. **Cover photo:** The background
photograph was taken by the Labor Community Strategy Center at its march and
rally at the Los Angeles Board of Education in 2016 demanding an end to the federal
program that provided military-grade weapons to LA's school police.

Library of Congress Cataloging-in-Publication Data
Names: Warren, Mark R., editor.
Title: Lift us up, don't push us out! : voices from the front lines of the
educational justice movement / edited by Mark R. Warren.
Description: Boston, Massachusetts : Beacon Press, 2018. |
Includes bibliographical references.
Identifiers: LCCN 2018005033 (print) | LCCN 2018005587 (ebook) |
ISBN 9780807015803 (ebook) | ISBN 9780807016008 (paperback : alk. paper)
Subjects: LCSH: Community and school—United States. | Educational change—United States—
Citizen participation. | Educational equalization—United States. | Minorities—Education—
Social aspects—United States. | BISAC: EDUCATION / Educational Policy &
Reform / General. | EDUCATION / Organizations & Institutions. |
SOCIAL SCIENCE / Discrimination & Race Relations.
Classification: LCC LC221 (ebook) | LCC LC221 .L54 2018 (print) |
DDC 379.2/6—dc23
LC record available at https://lccn.loc.gov/2018005033

To our young people,
the next generation of social justice organizers

CONTENTS

PREFACE

– Mark R. Warren and David Goodman –

MARK'S STORY

In February 2015, I was sitting in a room with a dear friend, Lori Bezahler of the Edward T. Hazen Foundation, talking about the tremendous response I had gotten to an article I published on the need for an educational justice movement. I said I had to find a way to build on this article—why don't I write a book about how organizers and education activists are building this movement today? Lori countered with a different approach; she suggested I work with them to tell their own stories of movement building.

I immediately saw this as a great idea. I would get to invite all of my favorite people—organizers and educators who I thought were doing exciting and groundbreaking work. And wouldn't it be more compelling and inspiring for readers to hear directly from movement builders themselves? I could bring these organizers and activists together to discuss their essays as part of this process. They could build new and stronger relationships in these meetings, and that itself would be a direct contribution to movement building. Our collective sharing and learning process would then be reflected in the book.

The plan struck a chord, and I received an overwhelmingly positive response from organizers and activists to participate in the project. People were hungry for a chance to share their stories, deepen their analyses of systemic injustice, discuss the lessons of movement building, and develop new strategies for organizing across sectors and movements.

Around that same time, I helped found the Urban Research-Based Action Network, a group of activist scholars trying to reimagine the relationship between the academy and community. We were looking for new ways of producing knowledge that did not always situate the professor at the top of a hierarchy. We wanted instead to lift up community knowledge and work in partnership with community and education activists. I saw the book as a way to reimagine scholarship as a collaborative process that directly seeks to advance social justice movements.

Sanjiv Rao from the Ford Foundation embraced this idea right away and helped shape and support it. Joined by another thirty or so movement builders, the contributors to this book gathered in December 2016 at the offices of the Ford Foundation. We met just after the presidential election, and that brought a new urgency to our convening as well as a stronger recognition of the need for organizers and activists to support one another across movements. Contributors shared ideas for their essays, and we engaged in deep reflection on both what we learned together and the challenges we face to build a larger, stronger, and more unified movement.

We made sure to create a space where movement builders could bring their whole selves. We shared art, poetry, and song. We wanted to be smart and strategic but also to express the care and love for young people and for each other that animates the movement and sustains our participation.

It was such a powerful meeting that participants wanted to meet again. We met six months later and decided to form a People's Think Tank as a learning community and an idea space for movement building. The network would use the book as a first step to promote intersectional movement-building strategies and engage new people in the struggle for educational justice.

During this time, I met David Goodman, a professional writer with a deep commitment to social justice. David became an invaluable partner in crafting this book. He gave me terrific advice about all aspects of writing and publishing. At times he pushed me to get out of my academic head and better orient myself to a larger audience. Along with me, David worked with most of the contributors on their essays.

Lift Us Up, Don't Push Us Out! represents the culmination of over twenty-five years of my engagement with community, parent, and youth organizing and with the broader educational justice movement. I have strongly shaped the contours and content of this anthology. Nevertheless, movement builders speak for themselves in their essays. They tell their stories and offer their analyses in their own voices. Together, I believe, we have produced a summary of the best of the last fifteen years of movement organizing and have highlighted models for organizing and educational justice that point the way forward.

DAVID'S STORY

In 2008, I met Chelsea Fraser, then a thirteen-year-old eighth grader from Brooklyn. She told me how police officers had come to her school to arrest her and four eighth-grade boys, handcuffing them and marching them out of the building in front of all their classmates.

Chelsea's crime? Doodling. She wrote "okay" on her desk in block letters.

At the precinct, Chelsea was handcuffed to a pole over her head for three hours. "Hard Time Out," my article about this incident, featured in *Mother Jones*, was one of the early published accounts of what has come to be known as the school-to-prison pipeline. That story and my conversation with Chelsea and her mom have always stayed with me.

White people are often shocked when I describe how police handle routine discipline in many schools serving communities of color. This reaction underscores the apartheid nature of education in the US, where white students have a vastly different experience of school than students of color. I saw a similar dynamic in schools in apartheid South Africa, where I reported from for many years.

I was excited when Mark invited me to work on this book. This book, and the educational justice movement that it lifts up, constitute an important effort to bring these two worlds together. I am moved and inspired by the ordinary citizens and activists who contributed their powerful voices and shared their stories with us for this book. They are our hope for the future.

BUILDING A NEW EDUCATIONAL JUSTICE MOVEMENT

– Mark R. Warren –

THIS BOOK FEATURES VOICES from the front lines of a new movement for educational justice that is growing across the United States. Each author tells the story of how black and brown parents, students, educators, and their allies are fighting back against profound and systemic inequities and mistreatment of children of color in low-income communities. These activists are advancing a vision for humane, high-quality, and culturally relevant education.

We desperately need a new way forward. Reforming traditional schools through high-stakes testing has hit a dead end. The charter school movement has been taken over by corporate-backed reformers who offer choice but no real improvement in educational opportunity. In fact, charter schools have some of the harshest discipline and highest suspension rates of all schools, while failing to educate children any better. We are stuck either defending public schools as they are or privatizing them.

The contributors to this book challenge both entrenched district officials in traditional public schools as well as school privatizers, because neither directly addresses the systemic nature of racism in our education system and in the broader society. The failures of public education are a profound racial and social justice issue. They must be addressed as such by building a broad social movement committed to educational justice. This book tells the stories of how parents, young people, educators, and their allies are building that movement today. It is a call to action for those who care deeply about the lives of all of America's children and want this country to overturn its history of racial oppression to become a land of opportunity and an inclusive democracy for all.

SCHOLAR ACTIVISM AND MY JOURNEY TO EDUCATIONAL JUSTICE MOVEMENTS

I first met the nascent educational justice movement when I began to study community organizing efforts in education reform in the 1990s. I was in graduate school getting a PhD in sociology from Harvard University and researching the Alliance Schools Initiative, led by Ernesto Cortes and the Industrial Areas Foundation in Texas. Most sociologists at the time studied communities "from above" and treated people's lives as so much fodder for sociological theorizing. While personally progressive, many of these sociologists were content to publish study after study showing the effects of racism, for example, but not do anything to address it. I was looking for a different approach. I believed we had a lot to learn from the people who were leading organizing efforts. I wanted to study the work of these people, lift up successful models, and also partner with them to contribute to racial justice and community power.

I had long believed in the importance of working people organizing to build power. I grew up in a white blue-collar family and neighborhood called Hungry Hill, in Springfield, Massachusetts. My mother was an ardent Catholic, daughter of Italian American immigrants. My father was a warehouseman, a New Deal Democrat, and an activist in the Teamsters Union who taught me the necessity for working people to fight for their rights. However, he was quite unusual for a white, working-class man at the time. He supported the civil rights movement and taught me that racism was wrong. His vision of working people uniting across racial lines for racial justice and a better life for all became my life commitment. I became radicalized in college and left to work as a labor and community organizer. I brought that experience and a commitment to building social justice movements with me to graduate school at Harvard.

I knew that working people and people of color had many issues to fight, but I cared about educational justice for personal reasons. I was the only boy in my neighborhood to go to college; public education opened up the world to me but not to my friends. They thought they were going to get well-paying factory jobs like their fathers, but just then factory after factory started to close in Springfield and across the country. My childhood friends have struggled ever since with unstable employment while I went to Harvard.

As I started to study organizing efforts, I learned that for African Americans and many Latinos, the struggle for education was not solely about economic well-being. It was bound up with the struggle for liberation, for political power and full citizenship, and for their very lives. This history goes back to slavery, when it was forbidden to teach black people to read, and runs through the citizenship schools of the civil rights era. When school failed black and brown children, they often ended up on the street and in jail, many even dead. Visiting Baltimore, I heard young black organizers in the Baltimore Algebra Project chant, "No education, no life." I learned the profound truth in that declaration: getting an education was truly a life-or-death matter for them.

Meanwhile, my oldest daughter entered an urban middle school in Cambridge, Massachusetts, and the racist treatment of children of color became personal to me. I had married a black British woman—Roberta Udoh, an educator whose essay appears in this book—and we had two beautiful black, biracial daughters. I saw her middle school come down hard with zero-tolerance discipline toward black students, suspending them and alienating many from school. The school-to-prison pipeline was no longer something I read about or heard about from people I met in my research. It was happening right in front of my eyes.

By this time I had just finished writing a book called *A Match on Dry Grass* with a faculty colleague at Harvard, Karen Mapp, and fifteen doctoral students, documenting community organizing efforts in six localities across the country. These were very important efforts to build leadership of parents and students and to create real change in schools and education policy at the local level. We treated these cases separately, as independent local cases, and that made sense at the time.

But something was changing by the time the book came out: a new movement was rising. Local groups were beginning to join together in various kinds of formal and informal alliances. While in 2008 there were almost no national coalitions, by 2015 we had the Alliance for Educational Justice, the Dignity in Schools Campaign, the Journey for Justice Alliance, and the Alliance to Reclaim Our Schools, as well as a web of networks across local groups and in various alliances with unions, advocacy groups, and other organizations committed to educational justice. In the past, the hunger strikers discussed by Jitu Brown in his essay would have fought the closing of Walter Dyett High School in Chicago on their own, or perhaps just with local support. This time they mobilized support nationally through the Journey for Justice Alliance, tapped connections in the American Federation of Teachers, and used social media to reach out internationally. They "nationalized" their local struggle, as Jitu says, creating the additional pressure on the mayor that helped the strikers win their campaign. In the end the hunger strikers inspired organizing efforts against school closings across the country, helping to create a larger movement against the privatization of public education.

The movement to combat the school-to-prison pipeline had also taken off by 2015. Consisting of multiple and overlapping local struggles, and organized into national coalitions like the Alliance for Educational Justice and the Dignity in Schools Campaign, the movement was driven by parents, youth, and community organizing. Young people of color had asserted themselves strongly in this movement, demanding a voice along with parents in creating justice for themselves. These grassroots organizations had managed to form large and interconnected alliances with civil rights and legal advocates, researchers, and educators to turn the tide of public discourse away from zero tolerance, win changes in school discipline policy at local and state levels, and help push the federal government to issue new guidance that warned against harsh and racially discriminatory practices and encouraged the adoption of restorative justice alternatives.

The title of this book, *Lift Us Up, Don't Push Us Out!,* and its accompanying graphic on the cover of the book, comes from the movement to combat the school-to-prison pipeline. The Dignity in Schools Campaign adopted the slogan and graphic for its Week of Action Against School Pushout, in 2016.

Increasingly, the various components of the movement began to connect. These connections were partly driven by the need to respond to the emergence of a corporate-led school reform movement intent on privatizing public education. These well-funded groups lobbied to get districts to close so-called failing public schools and open charter schools in their place. The closed schools were disproportionately located in low-income communities of color, which led the Journey for Justice network to file a civil rights complaint against them. While charter schools may originally have been a place for small-scale innovation and experimentation, often by nonprofit groups, by this time private management companies had come to dominate the charter movement, and they were not democratically accountable. Whole districts, such as New Orleans, had been converted to charter schools, and the threat loomed in Chicago, Philadelphia, New York City, and elsewhere across the country. Local organizing efforts on their own did not have the resources to defeat these campaigns. They needed support from a national movement. The educational justice movement has emerged to meet that need.

SYSTEMIC RACISM AND THE NEED
FOR AN EDUCATIONAL JUSTICE MOVEMENT

While studying the movement to combat the school-to-prison pipeline, I traveled to the Richmond, Virginia, area to visit Advocates for Equity in Schools and I Vote for Me, local organizing and advocacy groups fighting racially discriminatory school discipline policies, with a special focus on students with special needs. The morning after I arrived, I was scheduled to interview coleaders Kandise Lucas and Lorraine Wright. But I received a call from them at 11 p.m. They had to cancel the meeting because a distraught mother had just contacted them about a school security officer who had accosted her son outside his middle school that day. Kandise and Lorraine invited me to join them as they accompanied the mother to a meeting at the school the next morning.

I sat there in shock and anger as the mother recounted what had happened. Her African American son had an IEP (Individualized Education Plan) that specified he could take a break from class and get some fresh air out on the school grounds if he needed to. When he took a break that day, however, a security officer followed him outside, handcuffed him, and dragged him along the ground. The school sent him home, where he arrived with his clothes full of mud from the assault all the way down into his underwear. The vice principal called the parent and told her to keep him home for a few days. He wasn't suspended, an action that would have created a paper trail, but his mother was told she should keep him home nonetheless.

The mom faced an array of impassive school and district officials at the meeting. They had just watched a video that was taken of the incident but refused to show it to the mother. Although they agreed that handcuffing was wrong, none of the staff seemed to care that a child had been abused. No one apologized or offered to do anything to help. At one point, the district administrator got up from her seat and said she had to leave because "some of us actually have to work." The mother had, in fact, taken time off from her job to attend the meeting. In the end, the mother felt she had to accept the one hundred dollars the district offered to replace the young man's damaged clothing in exchange for her agreement not to pursue any further claims.

I have witnessed or heard story after story like this as I traveled across the country. The movement for black lives has exposed police brutality and killings on the streets, but black and brown children are being brutalized in schools every day and their families disrespected and bullied. In Los Angeles, I learned that police used to stand outside of schools and give students arriving late hefty truancy tickets. The costs would mount up to hundreds of dollars. When families couldn't pay, the students were arrested and many were sent to juvenile jail. I also learned that LA schools were so militarized that the district's police department owned a military tank. In Chicago I saw metal detectors and armed security guards everywhere; many schools had police stations located in the building. Meanwhile, most schools in the city lack art, music, and physical education classes, and there was no recess for children for decades.

These examples represent the tip of the iceberg of deep-seated and systemic racism in our public school system and in our broader society.[1] Children of color are far more likely to grow up poor than their white counterparts. Fifty years after the end of the civil rights movement, we have constructed a society in which nearly half of all black children grow up poor, many desperately poor and even homeless. They often live in neighborhoods that suffer from environmental degradation, violence, and police brutality.

Rather than providing opportunities for a better future for these children, public education has become part of the same system perpetuating racial oppression. Black and brown children from low-income families typically attend schools that are systematically underfunded, lack necessary social and emotional supports, have less-qualified teachers, and teach a Eurocentric curriculum that ignores their culture and history. The school-to-prison pipeline is perhaps the clearest example of the interlocking systems of oppression facing black and brown children. Harsh and racially inequitable school discipline policies lead to high rates of suspension; indeed, black children are three times more likely to be suspended than their white counterparts. The problem is widespread: 75 percent of all black students in Texas have been suspended. Children who are suspended are more likely to fail to graduate from high school and then end up on the streets and in the criminal justice system. Two-thirds of all black men without a high school degree end up in prison at some point in their lives—*two-thirds!* And one-third are in prison at any one time. Convicted felons are denied access to public housing, can be legally discriminated against in job hiring, and lose the right to vote in many states.

Unfortunately, many Americans recognize racism only at the individual level, when a person intentionally says racist things. However, the racism at play in schools is systemic, involving not only racist ideas but also policies, practices, and institutional arrangements that keep black and brown young people poor, uneducated, and criminalized. Racial stereotypes play a role in this system too, as, for instance, when educators label black boys as "troublemakers" or their families as "bad parents." An entire system based on white supremacy works to keep black and brown communities down and power and resources in the hands of affluent white Americans.

This is a profound issue of racial and social injustice. We know from history that entrenched systems of injustice can only be challenged through social movements, such as the civil rights movement. That movement overturned legal segregation, won voting rights and political power for African Americans, and vastly increased antipoverty and social programs that benefited millions of African Americans and many others across the board. As a result of the gains of the civil rights movement, the test score gap between black and white students closed substantially in the seventies and eighties, only to widen again as conservative forces regained power and began to cut social programs.

As you will see from these essays, the new movement that has been built over the past ten years explicitly names racism as the central problem in school failure and calls for strategies to directly address racial equity and justice. It has emerged as an educational *and* racial justice movement led by people of color.

THE STORY OF THIS BOOK: A TOOL FOR MOVEMENT BUILDING

Around the time that black parents in Chicago staged their hunger strike to save Walter Dyett High School, I published an article about the new movement called "Transforming Public Education: The Need for an Educational Justice Movement" in a free online journal. I received an immediate and overwhelming response, with the article quickly downloaded several thousand times.

As a next step, I decided to write a book on the subject that would include the voices of people building this movement in order to engage a broader audience on the need for addressing educational injustice and inspire others to act. I saw it also as an opportunity to bring these organizers and activists together, so the book project itself could be a way to help build the movement. Although many networks were forming across localities, organizers and activists often continued to operate mainly in their own sector. Collaborating on the book would be an opportunity to build relationships, lift up models of success, and tackle some tough issues. In the end, we would share stories, analyses, and lessons with one another across our sectors and then out to a broader audience in the education reform world and beyond.

I invited many of the organizers and educators I met in my research and activism to contribute to this book, people whose work I deeply respect and people from whom I have learned so much over the years. The response to my invitation was universally enthusiastic. The convening and book, like the article, struck a nerve and revealed the hunger to connect and build an alternative vision for racial and social justice in education.

THE PLAN OF THE BOOK: KEY COMPONENTS
OF MOVEMENT BUILDING

I organized the book into four parts, which cover what I believe to be key aspects of successful social justice movements. Each section includes the voices of leading movement builders addressing these issues.

First, successful movements are led by people who are the most affected by injustice, in this case students and their parents or families from low-income communities of color. Participation and leadership by students and families of color anchor the movement in their experiences, ensuring that the movement stays accountable to their needs. Parents and students also bring urgency to the demand for change. The essays in the first part of the book highlight the disrespect and pain inflicted upon parents and children of color from low-income communities. Yet in these essays we also see how participation in organizing efforts transforms parents and young people into powerful leaders of their communities. The essays also show the power that can be generated when parents and youth leaders work together in intergenerational alliances, as in the campaigns to end zero-tolerance school discipline policies and create restorative justice alternatives. Building a movement with strong participation and leadership of families of color is hard work, but the essays lift up models of some of our most successful organizing efforts and show the radical potential for change through building power among those most affected.

Parents and students cannot build a movement on their own, working in isolation in local communities. The essays in the second part of the book show how alliances can be built to connect organizing efforts across localities and to a range of allies. We see how national movements and allies provide critical support for local organizing. They also help "nationalize" these fights, lifting them up to inspire action in other places. The expertise of professional advocates, financial support from philanthropy, and the legal strategies of civil rights lawyers represent critical resources that help create stronger campaigns. Meanwhile, we also learn about important changes occurring in teachers' unions that have traditionally opposed demands for change by organized communities of color. Many are now joining the movement, with the Chicago Teachers Union leading the way to social justice unionism. Finally, we also learn in this section how a strong cross-sector alliance rooted in parent and youth organizing can achieve commitments from elected officials for large-scale systemic change in the form of community schools.

Parents, youth, and alliance builders can push for these kinds of changes from the outside, but creating new models of empowering education will require the work of educators on the inside as well. The third part of the book highlights the voices of educators who are leading change efforts in schools, school systems, and universities. We hear from teachers who are creating deep cultural changes in schools through restorative justice initiatives working in alliance with students and families. We also learn about the efforts by teachers to connect their community activism with classroom teaching and to create culturally relevant curricula that nurture the souls of black and brown children. We hear about how school board members can ally with community and labor organizations on the outside and work with district officials on the inside to create large-scale system change. Other voices address the transformations needed in higher education so that schools of education can prepare teachers for urban classrooms and become institutions that ally with communities in movement-building efforts. This requires a new model for scholars who reject the confines of the ivory tower and provide pathways for young people by connecting the classroom to the community.

The fourth section of the book includes essays from activists working to build a stronger and more effective movement by connecting educational justice to labor, immigrant rights, and LGBTQ movements. We are reminded that many workers are also parents who care deeply about their children's education and are finding ways to use their unions as a venue for parent advocacy. Meanwhile, we learn how the immigrant rights struggle is fundamentally an educational justice struggle and see methods to bring them together to build a stronger movement with a shared agenda.

The final essay by the contributors challenges us to take not just a cross-movement approach but an intersectional one as well. LGBTQ students of color are in many ways our most marginalized young people, as they are impacted by multiple systems of oppression at the same time. As a result, they are often out front as leaders in both the educational justice and LGBTQ movements. If we place the lived experiences of people with multiple marginalized identities at the center of our analysis and strategizing, we can create a movement that is fully inclusive and a vision for educational justice that empowers all young people.

In the concluding essay of the book, I highlight important themes that appear across the essays and that speak to the challenges we face in building a stronger and more unified movement. These themes include confronting deep-seated racism, building alliances rooted in the leadership of communities of color, tackling the profound mistrust that often exists between educators and families of color, and creating a vision and program for a truly empowering form of education for black and brown children. I end by discussing the potential of the educational justice movement to connect issues and communities fighting for economic, racial, and social justice and serve as the catalyst for a new social movement.

I am a white college professor writing about the struggles of low-income communities of color. Although I come from a working-class background and have a multiracial family, I have had many privileges connected to my race, gender, and current middle-class status. It has been an honor and a different kind of privilege to work with the organizers and movement builders in this book and beyond, most of whom are people of color. I have been warmly welcomed into this movement, and I take that as a profound responsibility on my part. I try to use my privileges and the resources I have to support and contribute to building the educational justice movement. It is now time for the movement builders to speak for themselves and share their stories in the essays that follow.

PART ONE

BUILDING THE POWER FOR CHANGE

Parent, Youth, and Community Organizing

1

‑‑◦‑◦‑◦‑◦‑◦‑◦‑

"I CAN'T MAKE A TEACHER LOVE MY SON"

A Black Parent's Journey to Racial Justice Organizing

– Zakiya Sankara-Jabar –

Racial Justice NOW!, Dayton, Ohio

Zakiya Sankara-Jabar describes how her African American son was pushed out of one preschool after another for minor behavioral issues. She formed Racial Justice NOW! to provide a voice for parents like herself facing racism in schools. In a few years, the group won a moratorium on pre-K suspensions in Dayton, Ohio, schools; changed the district's code of conduct to end zero-tolerance policies; won the implementation of restorative justice in ten schools; and issued school discipline report cards for school districts across Ohio. Zakiya reflects on what the experiences of black boys in schools tells us about antiblack racism in American society and the transformation of parents of color into movement builders.

MY INTRODUCTION TO RACIAL JUSTICE work grew out of my experience with my son in preschool. I was attending the University of Dayton, so I had access to its private preschool. Most of the African American children in the preschool had parents who were university students. I was upbeat and excited to have my son, Amir, on campus with me while I was attending school, and I felt safer knowing he would be close to me on campus. I wasn't political. I didn't think about race. I was just living my life, going to school, and working full-time.

The problems began right away. The preschool gave me a hard time enrolling him in the first place. Then in the first week, I started to receive phone calls from the preschool staff telling me, "He had a temper tantrum today. He's not wanting to transition from one activity to another."

"Is that not normal?" I replied. "Is that not something that your teachers can deal with?"

Then the preschool asked me to have Amir evaluated. Evaluated for what? It was as if he was a guinea pig. The staff told me, "We have a school of professional psychology here and they have students. They can come over with their instructor and they'll just observe him. They'll see if there are any services that he needs."

"Services? Evaluation? Psychology?" I responded. "What's wrong with him? Is he crazy?"

"We just feel like he's having some trouble transitioning," they said. "He's biting other students." They made normal three-year-old behavior sound very pathologized and abnormal. I realize now that I don't think we were ever really wanted there.

I felt uncomfortable about all this, so I went to see Amir's pediatrician. She advised me against doing the evaluation, because she worried that he would be labeled. When I reported this to the school, they were livid. It was as if I had broken some rule by getting a second opinion. Having preschool students evaluated seemed to be almost routine for them.

The preschool scheduled a meeting with me, during which they presented paperwork that was all ready for me to sign. I was told that if Amir had a disability or was identified as having something wrong with him, then he could go to a public preschool for free wherever I lived. It was as if they were selling me on this idea, like it was a win-win: we get him out of here and you don't have to pay, but he's labeled as a "problem child."

I refused to sign. I did my own observation. I wanted to see for myself what was going on. I saw that my son looked just like any other child in there. He was exhibiting the same behaviors as other children.

My pediatrician, who is an African immigrant, told me, "I've had the same problems with my son. If there are any other problems, come to me first." She added, "Your son is probably gifted. My son was gifted. They don't understand black boys or black children."

That's when the race question came up for me. I went to the university library and did a literature search about black boys and education. It turns out that there is a lot of research on the subject.

I suddenly realized that I wasn't a bad parent and my son wasn't abnormal. This was something larger, more societal, that was happening to African American parents. That's when I began organizing.

Meanwhile, the preschool threatened that if I didn't sign the papers, my son would be expelled. So I just took him out of the preschool, which meant I had to drop out of college. I decided to prioritize my son's needs.

SCHOOLS ARE NOT WORKING FOR BLACK CHILDREN

The data shows that schools are not working for black children, especially for black boys. A report by Learn to Earn Dayton showed something startling and heartbreaking: here in Montgomery County, where I live, black boys have the worst academic outcomes regardless of income.[1] Even black boys from more affluent families have lower third-grade reading proficiency scores and lower high school graduation rates than their peers, with poor black boys at the very bottom. That legitimizes the work of Dr. Jawanza Kunjufu and other scholars who have been saying for years that our children learn differently. In *Understanding Black Male Learning Styles*, Dr. Kunjufu explains that most black boys are hands-on, experiential learners, while schools emphasize visual-print learning; they are also kinesthetic learners, needing to move around a lot, while schools want students to sit quietly at their desks.[2]

I'm still dealing with the implications of these learning differences with my son, who's in fourth grade now. I'm trying to counter what he's hearing at school, where he's getting the message that "It's you—you're the problem. You were just born this way and you're not making it."

My son says, "Mom, I'm bad. I'm always getting in trouble." His trouble stems from the fact that he is a kinesthetic learner and needs to move around a lot. I found out from the other parents who had black boys with the same behavior or personality as my son—kids who are energetic, who know what they want, who have strong personality traits—that they had the same experience. I was coming to the realization that schools—regardless of whether they are urban, rural, or suburban—are not working for black children.

On the advice of Dr. Kunjufu, I put my son in an all-male school for kindergarten. The teacher was an African American male, an anomaly in

American education. When Amir started, I tried to prepare the teacher by telling him what my son was like. "He's energetic. He loves to move," I told him.

Days went by and I did not get a phone call. I thought something was not right—these people weren't calling me about Amir.

So I decided to stop by one day. I walked in and found the class loud and vibrant. They were learning the alphabet to a hip-hop DVD written by Nikki Giovanni, the famous African American poet. The kids were jumping up and down and clapping—"A, B, C!"

It was a class full of black boys in an all-black school, and the teacher was black. It was the total opposite of what my son and I had previously experienced. After things settled down and the children were transitioning to lunch, I walked with the teacher. I asked him, "How is Amir doing?"

"Oh, he's great," he replied. "He's one of my best students. He scored off the charts."

Nobody had ever said that about my son to me, ever. I still get emotional when I think about it. To this day, I think kindergarten was the best experience Amir has had in school.

Black children who are gifted, especially boys, often end up in classes for students with emotional disturbances. They get bored in school, the material isn't engaging, they get distracted, and they cause disruptions in class.

In *Countering the Conspiracy to Destroy Black Boys*, Dr. Kunjufu writes about the "fourth grade failure syndrome": by fourth grade, black boys have checked out of school. They don't like learning, because school has been traumatic for them.[3] I've seen that happen in my own son's life. I feel like white female teachers hate my son.

My husband and I are in a predicament: We both work, so we can't homeschool. We're just trying to make the public schools work for our children. The vast majority of parents like me are in a situation like this. As an active and supportive parent, I'm trying to change the school to make it more welcoming for children like Amir.

A HUMAN RIGHTS CRISIS

I ended up filing a complaint against the preschool with the Ohio Civil Rights Commission. I knew Vernillia Randall, who is now an emeritus professor at the University of Dayton School of Law. She told me that she didn't think I was going to get the result I was looking for and that cases like mine often take years.

Professor Randall offered another option. She said that we needed to organize. We needed to call a meeting and see if we could get other parents to join us to change policy. We needed to be explicit that this was a racial justice issue. That led to our founding Racial Justice NOW! in her living room.

Professor Randall and I divided up tasks. I organized and talked to parents, and she mined data and analysis. I had dropped out of school, so I used my time to go to my son's preschool and talk to parents during drop-offs or pickups. If they were black parents, most of the time they had some issue with the school—especially if they had boys.

As Professor Randall gathered the data and I collected the stories, it became clear that the bias and mistreatment of black children in schools is a human rights crisis that no one is talking about.

ORGANIZING FOR CHANGE IN DAYTON AND ACROSS OHIO

Racial Justice NOW! joined the Dignity in Schools Campaign (DSC), a national coalition of grassroots organizing groups and legal advocacy organizations. That was very important, because DSC had already done a lot of research and had resources for us to use. We adapted DSC's model code of conduct—which documents the harmful effects of harsh and racially inequitable school discipline policies and suggests alternatives, such as positive behavioral supports and restorative justice—and took it to the Dayton school board. We also held one-on-one meetings with the superintendent, the superintendent's lawyer, and the board president. I told my own story, and we brought along parents who had similar stories.

When we presented school officials with their own data that the district had reported to the state, they were shocked and embarrassed. We pointed out that Dayton was one of only three school districts in Ohio that were expelling preschoolers. Dayton's out-of-school suspension rate was four times the state average.[4]

We also found indicators of racial disparities. Black children made up 64 percent of the district's students but 80 percent of those suspended. Black boys with disabilities were the most suspended and expelled in the school district. While poor black boys were suspended the most, even middle-class black boys were suspended at higher rates than any other group.[5]

We received a lot of media coverage and made the front page of the *Dayton Daily News*. That's how we moved the ball as quickly as we did.

School district officials, perhaps because they were afraid of legal problems, started to pay attention and make changes. They acted on nearly all of our demands. They agreed to publish discipline data on their website so that parents could access it easily. In addition, the district implemented a moratorium on suspension for pre-K students, though they did not extend that through third grade as we had hoped. We had the zero-tolerance language taken out of the student code of conduct. They agreed to our demand to end suspensions for disruptive behavior, which is a catchall category for which most students were suspended. At the time, disruptive behavior was a level 2 infraction, which warrants an out-of-school suspension. We pushed them to change it to a level 1 infraction, where alternatives to suspension must be implemented first. Thanks to our efforts, the district agreed to stop suspending students for smoking tobacco and cursing. We won all these changes in one year.

The next school year, the district agreed to hire restorative justice coordinators for ten schools. We wanted coordinators because we heard that teachers did not know what to do with disruptive behavior and felt they lacked support for alternative strategies. The coordinators work with young people, create a special room where young people can take a break, and lead restorative justice circles with peers and the teacher if necessary. Restorative justice is an alternative to out-of-school suspension that seeks to repair harm and relationships. The following year, the teachers' union demanded that these coordinators be unionized teachers, so the coordinators became positive school climate teachers. In 2018 the district will add these teachers to ten more schools.

In 2016, Racial Justice NOW! successfully lobbied Dayton Public Schools to create an Office for Males of Color. Dayton became the third district in the country to establish such an office, after Oakland and Minneapolis. For the first time, the school district is going to focus on the experiences of black boys in a positive and constructive way.

The organization didn't stop there. We created discipline report cards for 1,100 school districts across the state of Ohio. We gave a letter grade to each district for their performance in three areas: the rate of suspensions and expulsions, with penalties for high rates of suspension in the pre-K to third grades and the seventh to ninth grades; the proportion of suspensions for reasons that are subjective evaluations, such as "disruptive behavior"; and the racial disparities in suspensions at all grade levels. Suspensions in pre-K to third grade are a serious indicator of harsh and racially inequitable discipline practices. And research shows that children who are suspended in ninth grade are twice as likely to not graduate as their peers, while almost 70 percent of black boys without a high school degree will end up in prison at some point in their lives.[6] In Ohio, 90 percent of school districts received a failing grade; only 6.4 percent of schools received a grade of B- or higher.[7]

Some of the superintendents in suburban districts were outraged about the report card. The schools in these districts normally get As on their academic report cards, but they received Fs on our school discipline report card, mostly because of racial disparity. These are schools that do not have a lot of children of color, but they disproportionately suspend and expel those that are there.

Racial Justice NOW! also helped to push House Bill 410, which decriminalized truancy in the state of Ohio. Previously, if children failed to attend school for too many days, the children and their families were referred to juvenile court. Now an intervention team works with the family first to determine the reasons for truancy and to find solutions.

When we began our work, no one was looking at the issue of the school-to-prison pipeline in Ohio. So not only have we organized and politicized our state legislators and local folks around this issue, but we've also helped our statewide policy organizations work on it as well. We're also seeing the impact of the report card on other school districts in the state.

The Dignity in Schools Campaign was the single greatest resource we had. DSC provided us with information and with useful resources, such as the model code of conduct. They connected us to opportunities to apply for small grants. DSC's field organizer visited us and helped provide our parents with training in organizing strategy. They gave us the chance to bring our voices to Washington, DC, when we participated in DSC's Days at the Capitol to lobby our congressional representatives on school discipline issues. Perhaps most importantly, DSC connected us to a network of like-minded groups in communities across the country. We could get advice from these other organizations and learn what worked and what didn't work. That has been invaluable for a start-up organization like ours that's led by young people and parents who are directly impacted.

BLACK PARENTS AT THE FOREFRONT

It's extremely important for parents of color, specifically black parents, to be at the forefront of movements for educational justice. We need more support for parents to come out of the shadows of shame and inferiority and break the negative stereotype of black parents. The myth of our not caring about our children's education needs to be shattered.

One of the ways we can do that is to help lift up the voices of parents of color all around the country. Their voices need to be brought out and cultivated. They need to be heard. That is what we are doing in Racial Justice NOW! and in the Dignity in Schools Campaign.

Sometimes organizations that advocate for black parents try to speak for them. But we need to have at the table actual parents who have experienced school failure and racial disparities and mistreatment firsthand. They should help inform policy. Their lived experiences make them experts. We need to speak up about what we know, what our needs are, what our demands are, and how we can make schools work for our children.

Teachers go into education because they love kids. They want to help students learn and reach their fullest potential. But because of the legacy of institutional racism and of dehumanizing blacks in this country, even teachers who want to help have their own biases. If you are a white teacher working in a school that is 99 percent black, how do you check those biases? Do you even want to?

I've tried to show my son's teachers that we are human. He has parents who love him and support him. He is not abnormal. He is not somebody you should be afraid of.

But I can't make a teacher love my son.

Amir is in fourth grade now, and this school year has been one of the most difficult. No matter what I do, I can't make the teacher see us differently. I can't make her love Amir. I can't make her see him as an energetic nine-year-old boy who has some leadership qualities that she could cultivate instead of viewing him as a menace or a nuisance.

One of the things I struggle with most is that there are no schools in this community—public, private, or charter—that work for my son. Living with that reality has been mentally draining. I feel that my work is not enough, that I'm not organizing enough people. I can never do enough, because I feel like the black community is in a state of crisis when it comes to education. I feel angry sometimes that there is not more outrage. We keep seeing these reports and this data, but nobody is up in arms. We need to make some drastic changes right now.

For the vast majority of our community, the abnormal has been normalized—that is, black children, especially boys, will routinely be suspended and labeled "failures" at school. I feel isolated because I refuse to let it be normalized. I know this is not normal. I know it is not right. I want to jolt the consciousness of our parents in our community to not accept the abnormal as normal.

2

⌁–⎓–⎓–⎓–⎓–⎓–⌁

#SOUTHLAPARENTLOVE

Redefining Parent Participation in South Los Angeles Schools

– Maisie Chin –

CADRE, South Los Angeles

Maisie Chin tells the story of CADRE, a parent-led organization dedicated to helping parents develop as powerful leaders in South Los Angeles schools. CADRE began through conversations among black and brown parents about the racist treatment of their children in South LA schools and how they felt disrespected by teachers and administrators. The group was one of the first in the nation to target the school-to-prison pipeline and name the systemic racism behind it. Maisie argues strongly for the need for parents to be at the heart of the educational justice movement, demanding dignity and respect. She challenges all of us to love the parents as much as we love the children.

FOLLOWING THE 1992 ACQUITTAL of police in the brutal beating of Rodney King, an unarmed African American man, which was caught on tape, South Central Los Angeles erupted in violence. It was the manifestation of decades of disinvestment from the region. I was an undergraduate at UCLA at the time and decided that I didn't want to perpetuate the dominant economic system and culture that pits people of color against each other. This led me to get involved in organizing efforts that forged my commitment to working for multiracial solidarity and unity.

After graduating from UCLA, I began working for an initiative that connected schools in key South Central neighborhoods across grade levels with the closest community college. Within a few years, however, it was obvious that we were going through the motions as far as equity, but we weren't doing anything to dismantle the stereotypes and the racism embedded in the culture of schools.

Teachers would stop me outside of meetings to express shockingly violent, dehumanizing beliefs about students and their parents. One white teacher invited me to agree with him that all of these children were "monsters." My goddaughter had this same teacher, who summarily failed everybody in the class except for one student.

This blatant contradiction between talking about equity and not connecting it to the implicit bias or outright racism in the classroom and toward parents led me to believe that we cannot improve educational outcomes in our communities without challenging the structural racism in our public schools.

This inherent disdain toward black and brown parents was a clear contrast to my growing up as a child of Chinese immigrants. South Central administrators and teachers would complain about black and Latino parents not showing up to meetings, answering a phone call, or returning some form. Meanwhile, my mom went to night school or worked the graveyard shift and did not attend a single parent-teacher conference after I was in third grade. Never was my family judged or my education denied because of a racist perception that we didn't care about education. It became clear to me at that point how families of Asian descent were being, and were allowing ourselves to be, used to perpetuate antiblack racism.

Racist perceptions of parents play a huge role in determining how schools respond to students. I started working on the modest idea that parents could be at the table to turn these perceptions on their head by sharing their wisdom and knowledge of their community, their children, and themselves. That's how CADRE (Community Asset Development Redefining Education) initially came about.

Conventional wisdom says that if you involve yourself as a parent of color, you can foster an equitable education for your child. The unspoken rule, however, is that you must never challenge schools or call out any of their practices as racist. That is the deal.

I met Rosalinda Hill, who cofounded CADRE with me, through a community project based in Watts. "Linda" was a parent with five kids who participated in every district workshop, conference, and training offered to parents. She was the one parent on staff at her children's school who served as the liaison between administration and the parents. Yet her son, who was in second grade and in special education, still got locked in a closet as a form of discipline.

She was extremely conscious of racism and very passionate about challenging people's perceptions about black boys in particular. In response to my modest proposal for parent engagement, Linda envisioned a movement of thousands of powerful parents. She realized that despite the years of her involvement as a parent volunteer, she had never been trained to be a leader-organizer, someone who could bring parents together as advocates for their children. Seizing on this new vision, she started organizing all of her friends. We met in her and other parents' living rooms every Friday night for two years, and in 2001 we launched CADRE.

PARENT EXCLUSION AS SYSTEMIC RACISM

Emotionally and spiritually, it took a lot of storytelling to show that despite what they did to be involved, South Central parents had no recourse to prevent mistreatment of their children. This had become too common an experience. You couldn't even say the problem was a lack of resources or books, or poor teacher training, or dirty bathrooms. Mistreatment was a symptom of a deeper problem: the fact that families and communities of color had no power and were not respected inside schools, despite having rights outlined in our state education code.

Rosalinda suggested we door-knock and ask parents if they felt they had power at the school. If they had the power, what would they change? If they had a magic wand, what would they change? Most of the parents we talked to felt completely disregarded by their children's schools. Without realizing it at the time, we equated fighting racism with challenging the treatment of black and brown parents.

We then started to ask ourselves: How do you make student and parent treatment into an issue? Can black and brown parents truly advocate for their children without backlash and retribution?

After two more years of house meetings and experimenting with different ways to bring attention to parent exclusion, we decided to start a participatory action research project and recruited a core group of parents to plan and carry out the effort. The majority were parents who had been incarcerated, whose children had been incarcerated, or whose family members had been incarcerated.

Our 2004 survey results made several things clear: the majority of the South LA parents we interviewed felt their schools were racist, did not recognize the culture and experiences of families, and had no real accountability to parents nor any meaningful form of parent engagement.

Meanwhile, stories kept coming up that revealed how systematically black and Latino parents' rights were violated and how these violations occurred most often during disciplinary proceedings. We started talking to lawyers and doing workshops for parents on the subject of their rights. We heard story after story. Students were counseled out of school or told to stay home for the rest of the semester. Some were told they had to transfer to another school, but the paperwork never went through, so they'd be sitting at home for two months. We heard how students became disengaged from school after these discipline incidents and about the domino effect that led to other negative consequences. And parents felt pretty powerless and angry.

PARENTS' POWERFUL QUESTIONS ASKED AND ANSWERED

By this point we knew we were going down a path less traveled but one inspired by history and political courage. We had these survey results and lots of stories. How were we going to use an organizing strategy to respond to what we heard?

The committee of core parents saw the power of our report's truth telling and wanted CADRE to use it for real change. We could have gone in many different directions. One parent, Roslyn Broadnax, said we can't just focus on *our* kids and fixing these separate incidents. It's not enough to help individual parents advocate for their child and settle for a few families getting a slightly better deal out of an unjust system. She challenged everybody to think about changing the rules of the game for *everyone*. By the end of two hours, she had organized all of us in CADRE to choose systemic change as our initial theory of change.

It was a watershed moment. The next question became, What's the system we're changing? The one our kids were actually living and experiencing, what our parents called the "school-to-prison train" that our kids were on. And what fueled it? Racially discriminatory school discipline practices that seemed to over-punish black children and then anyone whose behavior got close to antiblack stereotypes. But the system was also fueled by under-resourced schools, alienating school climates, poverty, and disinvestment in youth and community services in African American and Latino neighborhoods. Our parents' focus became stopping the "pushout" of students in all its forms.

There was one challenge: proving discrimination. The burden of proof in filing civil rights complaints is so high that it has left many parents of color frustrated. So we started investigating how we could apply a human rights framework to education. It was like a lightbulb went off. There was finally a name for all the pain parents felt. It went beyond suspensions to the deeper value of parents' lives and the lives of their children. Every negative experience students or parents had in South LA schools could be equated with a violation of a basic human right.

In June 2005 we adopted human rights as our framework and launched our Human Right to Education Campaign, naming three core principles: the human rights to dignity, a quality education, and participation in the institutions that shape our quality of life.

We began another participatory research project in the fall of 2005 in partnership with a human rights organization, the National Economic and Social Rights Initiative (NESRI). We went door-to-door to hold conversations with parents to find out if their children had ever been suspended; then we wrote down and documented their stories. We surveyed out-of-school youth and youth who were in alternative schools. We started to network with children's rights advocates, primarily special education lawyers.

This led to our "people's hearing" in June 2006, where we shared the extent and consequences of the human rights violations caused by zero-tolerance discipline policies and pushout. We had a great turnout of South LA parents, and we engaged attorneys and school board members to respond to testimonies. That day we also made our first public demand for a policy change.

THE CAMPAIGN FOR SCHOOL-WIDE POSITIVE BEHAVIOR SUPPORT

Several months before our people's hearing, we heard about the LA Unified School District's plan to adopt a new, more comprehensive school discipline policy. Some children's rights advocates inside the district were pushing for school-wide positive behavior support (SWPBS) as an alternative to harsh discipline. Under SWPBS, punishing students for negative behavior is a last resort; instead, school staff address the root causes of behavior and provide supports for students who need help. But SWPBS proponents in Los Angeles faced an uphill battle. People thought the plan was too soft. The teachers' union thought it took power away from teachers.

We had already excavated a gold mine of stories showing the need for SWPBS. While not as far-reaching as we wanted a new policy to be, SWPBS gave us the very leverage we needed. The new policy would require schools to look at and use discipline data to make and review disciplinary decisions and to be proactive so that suspensions became a last resort. Parents were to be included in designing each school's implementation. SWPBS would mean that everyone on all school campuses had to adopt positive behavior support practices. For once parents could begin to challenge discrimination in school discipline.

We threw our weight behind SWPBS. We went to school board meetings for eight months before our proposal came up for a vote, and we used the public comment periods to tell stories of families' experiences with pushout and its devastating consequences. We negotiated an additional policy component mandating that parents be included on the district-wide task force charged with independently monitoring SWPBS implementation.

The district's data also made the case for us by documenting the huge number of suspensions considered "normal" at the time. In 2005–2006 the district suspended nearly 73,000 students. In South LA some elementary schools suspended 150 students a year, while some high schools suspended 1,500 students a year. Meanwhile, nearly 40 percent of those suspended in South LA middle and high schools were African American students, even though they made up less than 20 percent of those schools' enrollments.[1]

Our family testimonies put human faces on these statistics and made great news stories that sharpened the debate and got out in front of our opposition. We organized support letters from judges, advocates, and civil rights groups around the country, applauding LA Unified for what it was about to do before they even did it.

It took nine months of mobilizing to overcome opposition from the teachers' union and others, but the school board finally adopted the SWPBS policy in 2007. We became one of the first community organizing groups in the country to win a district-wide policy shift away from zero-tolerance discipline and toward a more positive approach.

Our partner all along the way was NESRI, which, with CADRE and a handful of children's rights attorneys and community organizations like us around the country, helped start the Dignity in Schools Campaign, a national alliance committed to ending the school-to-prison pipeline. Our victory with SWPBS encouraged and excited advocates in the new alliance to challenge harsh and racist school discipline policies in localities around the country and to appeal to the federal administration in Washington to use its oversight powers to end such policies.

CHALLENGING THE POWER DYNAMIC
OF SCHOOLS VERSUS PARENTS

When individual parents of color challenge schools' treatment of their children, it often results in a deep power struggle that usually ends with the blame shifting squarely back onto parents: "You as a parent must be doing something wrong." We needed to shift the focus away from the parent's word against the teacher's—because the teacher always wins out—and turn this into a policy victory for systemic change. That's what we achieved with SWPBS, creating a basis and tool for parents to push back against the power of schools in discipline practices.

A district-wide policy doesn't matter, however, if it is not carried out or if no one has heard of it. That is why, after the passage of SWPBS, we placed a big focus on monitoring and evaluating implementation of the new policy and subsequent changes in school climate. We knew, then and now, that the political will to fully implement something like SWPBS would be hard to find in the high-turnover schools in South Central.

We spent a year working on community education. We helped parents learn to use SWPBS as leverage to help their children. We helped parents to see the value of being in solidarity with one another, because a positive school climate and ending racist school discipline helps everyone. SWPBS gives the school a shot at being a better place, with an "operating system" that is focused on preventing any student from being excluded from learning.

We conducted another participatory research project to find out whether SWPBS had been implemented with any fidelity in South LA. We performed our own independent analysis of the data and issued our first "shadow report" in 2010, followed by a report on "off the books" suspensions in 2012, and another shadow report in 2017. We continue to find that the more superficial aspects of SWPBS are being implemented, mainly to comply with district policy, and not out of a deep commitment to changing school climate and eliminating racially biased—namely, antiblack—discrimination in school discipline.

BUILDING SEEDS OF RADICAL LOVE AMONG PARENTS

To this day, and despite a 95 percent reduction in suspensions, we continue to train parents on how to monitor school discipline and school climate in their schools. It is at the core of our work to build the power we need for parents to confront the structural racism on which our schools are based. But building that power starts with the belief that black and brown parents' stories about school discipline and racist or unfair treatment matter. Many people in the general public or in schools react to these stories by thinking the parent is lying or blindly defending their child. It is where the division starts.

To this day, the most difficult political battle is creating space for these testimonies to happen in a transformative way. It's hard for parents to tell their story. It's hard to name discrimination at first, to not blame themselves. When parents share with each other, it's hard for them to be in solidarity with one another's truths, to not judge each other. Even so-called progressive folks often have a hard time not judging parents of color. It forces everybody to confront their biases. Validating parents' stories challenges the racist suppression of parents' voices and power, as well as the internalized oppression that fuels the idea of divide and conquer. It's where we start.

Our work involves building solidarity across parents' experiences in a nonjudgmental environment where people can look critically at these seemingly individual stories and identify the systemic issues across generations. We don't assign blame. We make the case, advocate, build consciousness, and find a common thread. The goal is to move beyond judging each other's parenting or children to seeing ourselves as a political force if we work collectively. We resist divisions among parents as much as we can, and we resist labeling parents as "good" or "bad." This is the greatest labor of love in our organizing model.

THE QUESTION FOR US ALL: HOW CAN WE AS A SOCIETY CLAIM TO LOVE CHILDREN BUT SO READILY HATE THEIR PARENTS?

This question continues to motivate our work. The narrative about "bad parents" hasn't changed despite our parent-led victories on school discipline policy around the country. We have shifted the narrative about discipline that justified the school-to-prison pipeline and caused zero-tolerance approaches to tumble and fall. Yet getting schools to accept, embrace, and love parents remains elusive.

Schools often "talk the talk" of parent engagement, so you don't see outright racism toward parents until they have to defend their children's humanity and behavior. You don't see it until it is a power struggle between the parent and the school—when school staff have the power of their unions, their professional status, and their elitist language behind them.

Our society believes that kids can be saved, so if we have to love somebody, we choose to love the kids. The more difficult struggle is to love and not give up on the adult who is their parent, to believe in the possibilities of a parent's continued growth and evolution.

In the work of education and racial justice, the challenge is the same: we don't ask ourselves to be as patient with adults. We pivot to the young people when parents are also in pain. Many parents haven't healed from the trauma of poverty and racism, possibly for decades.

Although black and brown parents like our CADRE leaders embody this history and trauma, they also embody all the possibilities for transforming our schools. It's going to be up to them. No one else has the skin in the game to do this kind of work—adult to adult.

Fundamentally, we are calling for a new paradigm of democratic schools that does not rely on getting rid of kids or parents to succeed. We believe our parents and all parents can be the shape-shifters. They are the ones who can and will call forth the better angels in our schools.

3

∘-∘-∘-∘-∘-∘

SPEAKING UP AND WALKING OUT

Boston Students Fight for Educational Justice

– Carlos Rojas and Glorya Wornum –

Youth on Board, Boston, Massachusetts

Carlos Rojas and Glorya Wornum tell the story of how students, as those most directly affected by injustice, are coming to the forefront of educational justice movements. Glorya, Carlos, and their fellow students have led campaigns to change the Boston school district's code of conduct to reduce harsh discipline practices, built a smartphone app to publicize students' rights and report unjust treatment, lobbied for state legislation to reduce suspensions, and led a walkout of over three thousand students to protest budget cuts to their schools. This essay shows how youth organizing creates transformational changes in schools and also transformational changes in the lives of young people.

GLORYA'S STORY

My experiences with schools always felt temporary. The label that's typically given to black and brown students is that we are bad students or unengaged. But I don't think I was unengaged. I felt like my teachers were unengaged with me, and that started the disconnect of my not wanting to learn or not being interested enough because I didn't feel like there was a real-world connection to what I was learning.

There would be times when we'd be in a classroom and I would ask a lot of questions. For example, I thought it was interesting that our history textbooks came from Texas. "Is this really history?" I would ask. I'd be seen as disruptive, even though I was just trying to figure out where our history was coming from and why it was coming from Texas. It would get to the

20

point where I was tired of a teacher telling me, "You're being disruptive; please go take a walk."

I didn't feel like it was disruptive. I felt like I was curious and wanted answers. What we were learning didn't relate to the struggles that I or my family was facing. I was considered disruptive because I was getting other kids to think about these things as well. No one taught me what to do with my frustration, so I would leave the class.

I began getting suspended from school in eighth grade. I think the discipline problems started with the inconsistency of my household. Sometimes people were there and sometimes they weren't, and sometimes things would get done and sometimes they wouldn't.

Ignorant people might say that mine is just a story of a stereotypical black family, a single-parent home, trying to figure out how to make ends meet or pay rent or work several jobs. But for me, because I was living through it, it was a struggle. It was hard to watch my mom be exhausted and have to cook dinner; my older sister would sometimes take me to school because my mom was too tired to get up and take me.

I didn't feel tough enough in my home, because I wasn't helping solve the problems. So I hung out with kids who I thought were tough. That's where a lot of my problems in school stemmed from: looking for something and not finding it at home or at school. So I had to figure out how to provide it for myself.

I would get into fights and arguments. I was suspended about twelve times. Once you're suspended for one thing, you get suspended for everything. You're suspended for a fight, and then you're suspended because you're asking questions.

It finally took my headmaster saying, "I really don't want to suspend you anymore. I really don't want you to be in trouble. I know you're not that."

I realized I was fighting the wrong way when I met people with Youth on Board, a national nonprofit organization that supports youth organizing. They helped me see that it's okay for me to have the energy that I do but that I should redirect it so that I'm fighting *for* something and not just fighting to fight. I started positively struggling instead of negatively struggling. I found positive energy among angry people. That was very different for me, because I was used to being around angry people with negative energy.

Now that I was surrounded by so many people who cared so much, I found what I was looking for.

Youth on Board allowed me to be angry and to feel what I was feeling. A lot of things need to be changed, and you're allowed to change it. They just told me "yes" so often. It was different. Before, everyone told me, "No, don't do that!" or "Be quiet!" or "Put your hand down!" Then I went into an environment where people said, "Raise your hand. Say something. Reach out to somebody. Be a part of something. Do something!"

It was important to have somebody guide me and say you can respectfully disagree and you can respectfully ask questions; it's okay that you're upset that your school isn't doing what it's supposed to. You get to voice those opinions. And you also get to make change with it.

CARLOS'S STORY

I was born in Colombia in 1993, and my mom moved to Boston when I was five. We came with tourist visas, which expired six months after we arrived. Then we became undocumented.

Because other members of my family were also undocumented, I grew up fearful of police enforcement and of anything that looked like the government. And I grew up watching family members both voluntarily leave and be involuntarily deported.

I was taught that I needed to behave and lay low, to impress and do well, and to speak eloquently and learn to not speak with an accent as quickly as I possibly could. Because of those messages, I became a student who mostly behaved well.

All around me I saw people getting in trouble for minor things. The police were always in the apartment building where I grew up. It seemed like every other day they were knocking on someone's apartment door. That was really scary and frightening to me.

When I was in tenth grade at Boston Latin School, I became involved with Youth on Board and the Boston Student Advisory Council. BSAC is made up of elected student leaders representing most high schools in the city. Youth on Board co-administers BSAC with the Office of Engagement of the Boston Public Schools. At Boston Latin, I saw disparities in school discipline that were based on race. That was the elephant in the room that nobody talked about. I started with a diverse class and I had lots of Latino friends, particularly men. By the tenth grade, many of them had been pushed out or transferred, because it was hard and they had gotten no support. I saw a very clear difference in the way students of color were treated: we were not supported to be in an academically competitive environment.

I became a student leader with Youth on Board, and school discipline was my campaign. It had everything to do with my experience involving immigration. Youth on Board and another group I joined, the Student Immigrant Movement, allowed me to make the connection between mass incarceration and the deportation of immigrants, and I saw how both of those systems work together to profit a certain group of private people. That angered me, because I watched family members being deported and friends and people that I knew being incarcerated.

When I was in the tenth grade, I was invited to a rally at Boston City Hall protesting budget cuts that were hitting the district. It was fully youth-led and all the speakers were young people. I was amazed that people as young as or younger than me were not just leading the rallies, but they had organized the planning meetings and decided campaign strategy too. I fell in love with that.

I'm undocumented and unafraid. It took me awhile to be able to say those words publicly at a rally in 2011 in front of the Massachusetts State House and the media. I had to make a choice between lying low, staying quiet, and focusing on school, or dedicating a certain part of my life to being public, speaking honestly about who I am, and speaking out against injustice and for educational and immigration justice. Youth on Board encouraged me and gave me the support to come out publicly at my own pace. I learned the power of public narrative and what it can do to change things.

THE POWER OF YOUTH ORGANIZING, BY GLORYA AND CARLOS

At Youth on Board we help young people understand the systems that impact their lives. Our organizing model brings in young people who have experience with the system. We help them to understand why certain things happen to them. So when they relate their personal experience—"I've been suspended X number of times," or "I've seen these things happen at my school"—they first see that they're not alone; then they see that these policies are part of something larger. The youth organizers and youth leaders at Youth on Board aren't just speaking about their personal experiences; they're speaking about an entire system and calling for change.

Code of Conduct and Chapter 222

Young people at Youth on Board have always brought complaints about what happened to them in school: "My cell phone got taken away." "I was suspended for having my phone out in class." "My teacher looked through my texts." The question always was, Is that allowed?

We started to address these issues by working with lawyers and advocates as well as parents through a group called the Code of Conduct Advisory Council. We called for changes in the Boston Public Schools' Code of Conduct, the school district's official policy related to student behavior and disciplinary actions. That turned into a massive overhaul of the code of conduct in the 2011–2012 school year, which is one of our biggest victories. We worked with the district to revise the code of conduct and make it one of the more progressive codes in the country.

Many codes of conduct in urban school districts dictate punishment first, based upon zero tolerance for any kind of disturbance or misconduct. That is what led to Glorya's experience of being suspended over and over again as a first and only resort.

We started advocating for the opposite approach: you don't solve a problem by suspending and expelling; you solve a problem with intervention, counseling, parent meetings, and tiered systems of support. We basically turned the code inside out. Instead of asking schools to resort to punitive measures first, the new code mandates that schools resort to punitive measures last.

Young people, parents, and advocates leveraged this victory to win a significant piece of statewide legislation in 2012 known as Chapter 222. This law mandates that all school districts across the state must try alternatives before punitive measures. The legislation says that schools must have an educational plan so that suspended students don't fall behind, that they must provide students with educational services if they are suspended for longer than ten days, and that they must provide special education services. The law also mandates that students have the right to due process if they're going through a suspension or expulsion hearing, that parents must be notified, and that serious attempts to involve parents must be made and documented.

Everyone involved brought something unique to the effort to win this statewide legislation. We were successful because every important stakeholder voice was included. We worked with legal advocates who had been in court defending young people, with parents who had fought to stop their children's suspensions, and with young people who had been directly impacted by the system.

Youth on Board and the most successful organizing groups believe that you cannot do something without having the people directly affected by the issue present and included. Teachers, parents, and legal advocates have important perspectives, but students are the ones directly impacted by these policies. We brought energy to this campaign because it's our lives and our education that are affected by these harsh policies.

Students and parents brought our stories to this campaign. It was critical for state legislators and district officials to hear and understand the real-life consequences of harsh discipline policies. We brought a parent whose son had been suspended close to twenty times while he was in kindergarten. Hearing from his mom about her experience as a mother helped move legislators to adopt policy change.

People understand narrative; people hear things through stories. The best way to get people to change is to tell our stories and speak to values. That's what's so powerful about youth organizing in dismantling the school-to-prison pipeline: we're able to tell our stories and speak to the values that a lot of us in this country hold about fairness and equity and about second chances.

An App for Student Rights

In 2015, BSAC created a Boston Student Rights smartphone app. In its first two years, it was downloaded over thirteen thousand times and used over twenty-three thousand times. The app includes a list of student's rights and provides information about policies that students often get suspended for violating, such as the dress code and setting off metal detectors. The app has a reporting feature, so students can report an injustice to the district office. But before they take that action, the app suggests alternatives to try, such as connecting with a teacher or supportive adult, and it provides phone numbers to call for help.

The app is a way to help implement real change and hold systems accountable. We've had situations where some of our leaders were about to get disciplined or suspended, and they were able to whip out the app and say, "Not so fast. This is the new code of conduct." The administrator acknowledged the rule or correct procedure and then backtracked on the disciplinary action. In other cases, students have been able to report a grievance and say, "Here's where I think my rights were violated." The district receives that data and in some instances has been responsive to addressing the conflict.

This app isn't just for students. It's also for administrators, teachers, and anyone involved with student behavior. We've learned that you can change the policy, but if people don't know about it, it might as well have not changed at all. Large school districts don't have an effective way of informing people about policy changes—especially changes that reflect big cultural shifts. So the app has been helpful to teachers, who now have a useful summary of what the new code is, what they're allowed to do, and what they're not allowed to do.

Students Walk Out Against Budget Cuts

In January 2016 the mayor of Boston, who controls the school district budget, announced a series of massive budget cuts, with many impacting the high schools our students attend. The schools would have to lay off teachers, limit class offerings, and cancel important programs. Young people already felt the district did not adequately support their schools, and this round of budget cuts was the tipping point.

On social media a group of students called a citywide student walkout to protest the budget cuts. They wanted to let the mayor know that students were not going to accept the cuts. The call for a walkout caught on like wildfire. In early March 2016 more than three thousand students walked out of their schools, creating the largest student walkout in Boston history. Students rallied at Boston Common and then marched to the state house and city hall.

The walkout brought media attention, including an article in the *New York Times*, and created enough of a political crisis that the mayor shifted some funds back to the high schools. Then there was a second walkout when we said, "That's not enough; where's the rest of the money?" Students also stood up for their younger brothers and sisters and said they did not want cuts to elementary schools either. We had a meeting with the mayor, and he reinstated another $5 million to the schools. So the walkout created a shift in the power dynamics in the city that no amount of student testimony, parent testimony, or advocates telling the mayor to increase the budget had successfully accomplished. In the end some budget cuts still happened, but they were mitigated by the massive walkout.

Students at the Center of the Educational Justice Movement

Students need to be at the center of every conversation about public education, where everyone can see and hear them. We have a BSAC shirt that says, "Ask us—We're the ones in the classroom."

Nevertheless, young people cannot fight for educational justice alone. We need parents, teachers, adult advocates, and people who care. But adults cannot do this work under the assumption that they know better than young people, which they often think they do. We call that "adultism."

Adults might have more experience and organizing wisdom than young people, and that's important to share. But adults cannot think that they know more about the struggles of young people in education or that they can verbalize them better than the young people can. If we can get on the same page about that, we can start creating spaces that are intergenerational, where we're side by side but young people are front and center in the movement.

A perfect example of this is what happened during the walkout. Youth organizers dictated the issue they wanted to address (budget cuts), they dictated the tactic they wanted to use (a walkout), they dictated the target (the mayor), and they dictated the demands. Adults were then able to follow their lead and structure themselves to support the walkout and help make it successful. That is the kind of space we need to create in the educational justice movement if we're serious about centering young people and tackling adultism.

In addition, if we're hoping to build a mass movement, we must create organizational cultures that look and feel better and more human than what is currently out there. People will not keep coming to meetings and actions unless that space is warmer and more human than what can be found elsewhere.

That's one thing that young people are incredible at doing: creating movement spaces that feel like homes. That's one thing we can teach adult organizers.

EPILOGUE: GLORYA'S REFLECTIONS

I graduated two years ago from high school and had a baby, yet I still came back to organize. Youth on Board is a group of people who make you feel amazing. No matter how hard the fight is, there's just such a positive bubble and reassurance that, even though it's hard, we're going to get through it. Even though it's a big fight, we're going to break it up into little fights and we're going to get to our goal. It always feels like we're moving forward.

Being a part of Youth on Board helped me get on track to becoming the person I am today and the person I want to see my son become. Being a youth organizer makes me want to be in everybody's face all the time, but in a positive way.

I'm not a stereotype. I'm a leader. That's all I want to say.

4

FIGHTING FOR GENDER JUSTICE

Girls of Color Assert Their Voices

– Kate McDonough and Christina Powell –

Girls for Gender Equity, New York City

The experiences of black and brown girls as victims of school pushout and discrimination based on race, gender, and sexuality are often hidden. Kate McDonough and Christina Powell talk about the Schools Girls Deserve campaign, which involved one hundred girls in naming institutionalized racism and sexism within their school system and offering their own solutions to school pushout. The authors give examples of the kinds of discrimination that girls and gender-nonconforming people like themselves face in schools and call for practices that are fully inclusive to young people of all gender identities. The authors also discuss how young people of all gender identities can grow into critically minded and empowered leaders in their communities.

KATE'S STORY

As someone who identifies as trans and has a nonbinary gender identity, I was first drawn to organizing for gender justice because of how important it is for me personally. When I was in kindergarten, teachers had a hard time understanding and accepting the way that I expressed my gender. To them, I was not feminine enough. They would constantly talk to my parents about it instead of about how well I was doing at school. It was always "Well, no one can tell Kate's gender. If you're not careful, Kate's going to grow up to become a lesbian. We think Kate has some kind of gender confusion." If any young person picked on me, it was always framed as my fault, not something the teacher should deal with to make the class more accepting of me.

I was constantly chased out of bathrooms by my peers. I never got support from my teachers, so it reached the point where I absolutely hated going to school. Being there made me feel ill, and sometimes I faked being sick in the middle of the day so I could leave. Thankfully, I had the opportunity to transfer to a different elementary school where I was more accepted and began to thrive.

I grew up in the Bronx, and I was one of few white kids in my class at school. Even though my kindergarten teachers saw me as this weirdo, they also still saw me as smart—so smart that they even wanted me to skip a grade. It wasn't the same for some of my peers of color who are gender-nonconforming. I recognize how systems of oppression work and how, in many ways, being white saved me from being pushed out. If you're white, you can still be weird and smart.

What I love about Girls for Gender Equity (GGE) is how intentional we are about identifying and calling out institutionalized racism, sexism, homophobia, and trans phobia. We make sure that those who are the most marginalized and most impacted are at the center of our work and are driving it.

GGE has taught me a lot about what accountability in action should look like. There are moments when, as an adult staff member, I'm in spaces where our young people can't be, such as a meeting in Albany during school hours. I have to be accountable to advocate for what girls have said they want. I have to show up in solidarity. So when folks are being sexist and racist in their policy making, I can't be afraid to call that out and push for what our young people want. GGE has made me much more unapologetic in these spaces, where in the past I've maybe played it a little safe or tried to be more diplomatic. GGE has helped me become a little bit more radical.

At the same time, I've learned how important it is to lead with love. I love our young people so much, and I love people in the communities that we're in. The more I'm in a place of love and creating loving environments, the more centered I am, even in the toughest of times.

CHRISTINA'S STORY

I attend a very diverse high school in Brooklyn. There are Muslims, Caucasian people, and African Americans. But girls of color have a serious problem of pushout at our school, like at many others.

Girls mostly get pushed out because of their race. Girls' clothing is an issue, like when they're told that their style is "ghetto." Girls of color might be labeled as ghetto because of the way they act. Others may perceive them as ghetto because of the way they dress, their sense of their body, and how they speak.

When a teacher labels a student "ghetto," it is discrimination based on (1) the student being a woman, (2) the student's race, and (3) a teacher's perception of who the student is. Teachers will say things like "This student doesn't speak properly," or "Her clothes are inappropriate." Such statements are code for racism.

This labeling is also sexist: a woman can't wear a skirt because she's told it is inappropriate, but a guy can walk around with a "wife-beater" shirt and nobody says anything. Girls of color get harassed about their appearance and end up getting pushed out of school because of that.

For example, my friend came to school wearing boots and a sweater with graffiti writing on it. The teachers said it was inappropriate and made her take off her sweater. But a guy came in with a sweater that talked about gangs and guns, and they didn't tell him to take it off. It was unfair.

In our school, our principal keeps pushing us to wear uniforms, because, he said, our uniform represents our school. But I have my own sense of style. I don't want to be somebody that I'm not. It's just not right.

We formed a group in GGE called Sisters in Strength to support one another and push for change. We launched the Schools Girls Deserve campaign, in which we talked about school pushout. We created posters, and we made a replica of a metal detector so that people will understand what kids go through as they try to get an education. We also called for gender-neutral bathrooms for people who are uncomfortable identifying their gender, as well as better food, better activities, more clubs, and just more understanding of people.

In GGE we discuss social justice issues that affect the world and society and how we can change it. For example, we learn about educational justice, what it is, and how it affects children. We look for better outcomes. We organize events like the Schools Girls Deserve campaign to spread the message about what children in school go through and how their lives may change if their education is stopped for some reason. Participating in these events gives me more experience and knowledge about how these social justice issues affect society and how we can try to change it.

I think it's important for girls and students of all gender identities to be involved when education decisions are made. Everyone should talk about what's going on in their schools, what's similar and what's different, and how they can create better conditions where students feel like they aren't harassed, discriminated against, or racially profiled. We should have events or create clubs for teenagers to speak their minds and opinions on what's going on in school and how they want to fight for a better education.

Before Sisters in Strength, I was just a typical teenager who didn't know about social justice issues. Sisters in Strength made me a better person, one who is more knowledgeable and ready to stand up against injustice. As an active member of the group, I learn information that I share with my friends and fellow students and that makes them more aware and more involved as well.

FIGHTING FOR GENDER JUSTICE, BY KATE AND CHRISTINA

GGE is an intergenerational grassroots organization based in Brooklyn, but we work throughout New York City and also at the state and national level. The mission of GGE is to ensure, through organizing and education, that girls and women—including trans young women and gender-nonconforming people—can live self-determined lives. We run the Sisters in Strength youth organizing program, of which Christina is a part, which is a two-year paid internship for high school–age young women of color where they learn about social justice and engage in campaign work, with a focus on how girls of color are pushed out of school.

Sexist and racist perceptions of young women of color lead to their being disciplined for what they wear, how people perceive the way they speak, or how they show up in school. Young people are also critical of the curriculum. Many girls say they do not see themselves in the curriculum. They don't see women of color or learn anything about their histories. Trans women don't even exist in the curriculum, or if they do see themselves, it's usually from a negative perspective.

Concerns about policing and school metal detectors are a constant. One young woman missed her first-period class when she was stopped because the pins in her hair were making the scanner go off. She was told,

"Either you get in trouble or you take out your pins and mess up your hair." It's a racist and sexist way of disciplining young people; having your hair wrapped with pins isn't something that white girls do. She refused to take out the pins, so she missed her class and got in trouble for it.

Sexual harassment is totally normalized. When young women are being harassed, they often don't report it, because they feel like nothing will happen. The school doesn't know how to respond to it. This also can lead to pushout, because sometimes girls are being sexually harassed to the point that they fight back, and then they get in trouble for that. This is how institutionalized violence and the big issues of racism and sexism become cemented into everyday interactions in school.

GGE did a participatory action research project on sexual harassment in schools where girls in the group asked other students about their experiences. We found that when young people responded to harassment by standing up and fighting back, they tended to be the ones getting punished. The school looks at what's happening as the root cause instead of seeing it as a symptom of a bigger issue.

The Schools Girls Deserve

We captured the ways in which girls, transgender, and gender-nonconforming youth of color are pushed out of school and the vision of the school they deserve in our report called *The Schools Girls Deserve*.[1] We included over one hundred New York City girls and gender-nonconforming youth of color in the participatory-action research project that informed the report.

As part of our Schools Girls Deserve campaign, we created an activity where folks walk through two different kinds of schools. In the "pushout school," participants have to walk through metal detectors to experience how it feels for students who face this indignity every day. In the school that girls want and deserve, there is a curriculum that includes women of color, where girls can see themselves. In this curriculum they can learn about their own history and culture instead of hearing the typical Eurocentric, colonialist perspective. This kind of curriculum gives girls of color a sense of power and agency in their lives.

We have also pushed for culturally competent sex education that includes the needs of LGBTQ students. Our curriculum talks about relationships, power, and privilege and allows for young people to think through their identities. We also advocate for sex education that addresses sexual harassment and consent.

We have more police officers in our schools than we do guidance counselors and social workers. So we have also campaigned for more teachers and support staff and folks who understand the lives of girls of color and gender-nonconforming students. We need to look at how teachers of color are also pushed out of school.

We are also making demands for basic resources, such as clean drinking water. Many of our young people talked about how they can't drink from the water fountains because of lead contamination. They also talk about their desire to have a healthy or halal lunch.

Making a Difference for Girls

GGE has had several key accomplishments. In the past, school pushout tended to be framed as something that affected only young men of color. We've highlighted how school pushout is both a gender justice and racial justice issue. Ensuring that our young women have the opportunity to speak truth to their experiences is a major win.

Another accomplishment is the leadership growth of our young people. These young women now say, "This is not okay," and, "I know what I want and need and deserve." That's a major success.

Looking at educational justice through a gender justice lens is essential. When we do that, we see issues around sexism in the dress code, the normalization of sexual harassment in schools, and the lack of culturally responsive curriculum in which women are included.

In our own educational justice movements, we need to examine how we may unintentionally recreate the oppressive structure that we're trying to tear down. For example, to provide a safe space for trans young people, we need to do more than learn people's personal pronouns and use them; we also need to make sure there are gender-neutral bathrooms available. How do we make sure our own gatherings reflect the schools and communities we are fighting for?

Young people especially want to claim their gender identity for themselves and be recognized with appropriate pronouns. That could be the typical he/him/his or she/her/hers, but it can also be nonbinary like they/them/theirs or in other ways. Pronouns are important because it shows who people are. Pronouns are about identity. We teach people that it's important to ask what pronouns other people prefer, and use those pronouns. Doing so shows that you respect who they are and that you care about and support them. This kind of culture change can be hard, especially for many older folks, but we believe it is crucially important to creating an inclusive movement.

Public education does not need to be bankrupt or oppressive. We can create good, wonderful public schools for young women of color and gender-nonconforming youth of color. It's just a matter of prioritizing.

We need to trust girls and gender-nonconforming youth to be experts in their own experiences and to know what they need. Then it's the job of adults to partner with young people to help meet those needs and make our shared visions a reality.

5

⊸◦-◦-◦-◦-◦-◦-◦-

THE FREEDOM TO LEARN

Dismantling the School-to-Prison
Pipeline in the Southwest

– Pam Martinez –

Padres & Jóvenes Unidos, Denver, Colorado

For twenty years, parents and young people have been working together through Padres & Jóvenes Unidos to stop the school-to-prison pipeline and end the oppression of Chicano, Mexican, and Indigenous communities in Denver and beyond. Parents started organizing to stop a school principal from punishing Spanish-speaking students by forcing them to eat their lunches on the cafeteria floor. In 2008 youth leaders became the first in the nation to win a district-wide commitment to end zero-tolerance discipline practices and move toward restorative justice. Pam Martinez talks about the power of the group's intergenerational model to combat the racial oppression of Chicanos and Mexicanos in the colonized Southwest, and she recognizes that youth are the most fearless at leading the charge.

IN 1982 THE US SUPREME COURT ruled in the landmark *Plyler v. Doe* decision that schools cannot deny a free public education to undocumented children living in the US. My husband, Ricardo, and I had been involved in the historic suit when we were organizing for immigrant rights in Houston. Following that victory, we moved from Houston to Denver and continued our organizing for Chicano and Mexican rights.

One day while watching the evening news, we saw parents in front of the headquarters of Denver Public Schools with signs saying that their kids had been forced to eat on the floor as a form of punishment for speaking Spanish at Valverde Elementary School. The injustice was obvious. The parents said, "Anybody who can help us, please come on down and join us. We need your support."

Ricardo and I immediately joined the Chicano and Mexican parents and became part of the committee to help replace the white principal, since she refused to change. It was a tough fight. The principal was not only punishing students for speaking Spanish, but she also fired a national award–winning bilingual teacher who protested the practice and spoke to the kids in Spanish when needed. It took us a year, but the parents succeeded in removing the principal, rehiring the teacher, and ending a racist and humiliating form of "discipline."

THE DEMAND FOR RACIAL EQUITY

That was the start of a long journey to understand how deeply institutional racism manifested itself in public education. The demand for racial equity has been at the heart of this journey. Placing parents and students of color in leadership of these struggles has proved critical to improving education for Latino and other students of color in Denver and Colorado over time.

The struggle at Valverde inspired Chicanos throughout Denver to stand up and fight for their kids' rights. People started calling us from all over asking for our help. That was the birth of Padres Unidos, or Parents United, in 1992.

Padres Unidos became well known as an organization led by people of color from the community that openly fought racism and won. After we filed and won a complaint against Denver Public Schools with the federal Office for Civil Rights for violations of civil rights policies, parents at Cole Middle School on the east side asked us to help them organize. Nearly all students at Cole were Chicano or black, and almost all lived in poverty. A long-standing member, Pedro Herrera, invited us to his house along with about fifteen to twenty parents to hear the testimony of Cole students. When we arrived, there was a line of students out the front door, on the front porch, and down the sidewalk. The parents had brought students who were repeatedly being suspended at Cole for minor misbehavior. They told us, "Our kids are missing too much school. They're being sent home and missing instruction. They are not learning."

These parents were not against discipline in and of itself. They were against their children missing learning time as a form of discipline. These were immigrant parents who had fought to get into this country and were determined that their children would get a good education once they got here.

That night, the parents introduced us to a key feature of the school-to-jail track: the enormous number of kids being given out-of-school suspensions for minor misbehavior. We learned that the students missed classes so often that they fell behind. They were embarrassed to find themselves unable to understand what was going on in class and, as a result, would drop out. But we called this practice "pushout" to show where the blame belonged.

As parents organized, Cole students got involved too and asked to meet on their own. They said, "We can't really disagree with our parents in public. It would be disrespectful. We need a space where we can express ourselves and have input. We want to be part of Padres Unidos but have our own space. We will call ourselves Jóvenes Unidos." So our organization became Padres & Jóvenes Unidos (P&JU), or Parents and Youth United.

FIGHTING PUSHOUT AT NORTH HIGH SCHOOL

During this time, P&JU was invited to a conference hosted by a new national civil rights group called the Advancement Project. At this conference we learned that school pushout was happening across the country and was part of a larger systemic form of oppression for black and brown youth that included over-policing and criminalization of youth of color. Further research revealed a massive surge in the incarceration of young people of color. That was groundbreaking for us. It was the first time people named the school-to-prison pipeline and the systemic and institutional racism that it represented.

In our view, the unnecessary and racially disparate discipline of students of color was a primary obstacle to achieving the freedom to learn in the United States. It represented a continuation of the historic oppression of people of color in this country. Our experiences with school suspensions at Cole and the broader analysis of the school-to-prison pipeline would shape our organizing for the next fifteen years.

With our first substantial funding from the National Council of La Raza, we opened an office located near North High School, a historic school for Chicanos and Mexicans from the barrio. In 2003, Northside mothers and members of P&JU started telling us, "Our kids don't want to go to North

High School. They are depressed. They pretend they're sick in the morning. They'll do anything to get out of it and we don't know why."

So parent members decided to survey the students to get to the root of the matter. Students at North loved the survey and took it on as their own. They ended up collecting more than seven hundred surveys and analyzed the survey findings. Using what we call the "Padres Approach" framework, they identified the problems, analyzed the root causes, and developed concrete solutions to reform North High School, which they published in *The North High School Report: The Voice of Over 700 Students.*

The report told a powerful story. Many students felt that the atmosphere of the school was like a prison. They felt that discipline was unjust and that teachers did not believe in their ability to learn and go to college. This groundbreaking report showed that while over 93 percent of all students at North wanted to go to college, only 38 percent even graduated from the school.[1]

The students compared North to affluent white high schools within Denver Public Schools and revealed vast differences in the number of Advanced Placement classes being offered, graduation rates, and the number of students successfully attending and graduating from four-year colleges. The students filed requests under the Freedom of Information Act to obtain the data from the district and used it to support their campaign.

The North students held a press conference to release the report, demanding the reform of North into a college preparatory high school for all and other changes. Young people had never done anything like this before in Colorado, and it caused a sensation. The press conference led to front-page stories in both major newspapers in the area and was covered by thirteen media outlets. The impact of this work was tremendous. The struggle went on for a number of years, eventually leading to new leadership and to the reform and reorganization of North High School.

ENDING THE SCHOOL-TO-JAIL TRACK

But there was a larger problem. You can offer college prep for all students, but if high numbers of black and brown students are suspended and pushed out, they're not in school taking these courses; they end up railroaded into correctional facilities.

As a result, youth leaders in P&JU began calling for a change in Denver Public Schools' discipline code. They wanted restorative approaches rather than punitive practices. The youth pressed their demands at every school board meeting, issued press releases, publicized stories of disciplinary injustices from students and their parents, and held direct actions. We met weekly with Denver Public Schools, its attorney, and different stakeholders from the district, including the teachers' union, to negotiate changes in the code. We got further support from the Advancement Project, a Washington-based civil rights organization, whose attorney helped us to negotiate with district officials and suggested much of the language in the new discipline code. We learned that strategic partners like the Advancement Project could be critical to the struggle when rooted in the community's demands and direction.

On the day that the school board was going to vote on the new discipline code, the teachers' union said it could not sign off on the code due to member objections. As a result, it took another year and a half of negotiations to pass the new discipline code!

The code we won in 2008 focused on keeping students in school and learning. The policy was designed to eliminate racial disparities in discipline by using restorative justice practices that tried to get at the root causes of behavioral issues and support students as well as teachers and administrators to resolve conflicts rather than push students out.

This was a huge win nationally. It was the first time that a grassroots organization led by people of color got an entire district to change its discipline code, and we were invited to conferences and meetings across the country to share our experience. P&JU youth leaders traveled to Washington and spoke to the US Department of Justice and the Office of Civil Rights at the Department of Education.

The youth followed this victory by raising the bar even higher, seeking to end zero tolerance throughout the state. It turned out that the new district policy conflicted with state law. Youth leaders spent two years crafting legislation and lobbying for it at the state capitol. They strategized with legislative sponsors, testified at committee hearings, and mobilized their peers to rallies. Everyone came wearing our red T-shirts. We stood out. Here came the youth in red who were fighting to make change!

Members learned to use the press strategically to educate the public and pressure decision makers. We consistently messaged that the bill was meant to end racial disparities in discipline using restorative practices. While initially hesitant to discuss race explicitly, by the end of the two years, the press, TV reporters, the superintendent and legislators were all using our message. Our framing on racial disparities in discipline became the popular frame. This was intentional and a win.

In the end, our organization was seen as a pit bull. We did not give up. We were there for the duration and they could not shake us off. Those most affected demanded equity, respect, and equal time. By the end of this battle, significant numbers of parents and students had become freedom fighters for racial justice and educational equity for all.

It took two years, but the Colorado Smart School Discipline Law passed in 2012, another historic victory that inspired local organizing groups across the country to consider state legislation to end zero tolerance and help halt the school-to-prison pipeline. But these wins begged the question of how they were going to get implemented. People must learn how to hold those in power accountable for a real democracy to blossom and survive. It is part of realizing self-determination and justice.

We started producing annual school-discipline report cards, which parents and youth used to give grades to school districts throughout Colorado on the results of new discipline policies. This required collecting data, interviewing students, and gathering stories. The report cards became news items. Who was being called out? Which districts were improving? People wanted to know. And both district and school leaders started to want better ratings. In the end the report cards have helped push the state, districts, and local schools to change deep-seated institutional practices of racial discrimination and inequity. Our campaigns and new policies have made a difference: out-of-school suspensions for students of color in Denver fell by 58 percent between 2003 and 2013.[2]

POLICING THE POLICE

Our next campaign was to limit the overuse of police in schools and reduce their presence. Police had become so prevalent in schools that they were being involved in minor behavioral issues, which has never been their job.

Too many schools would send a police officer into a classroom to pull a student out in front of their peers and in some cases handcuff them for nonviolent, low-level misbehavior.

Students in Jóvenes organized to convince the Denver Public Schools and the Denver Police Department to sign a new intergovernmental agreement in 2013 to end unnecessary student referrals to law enforcement, to eliminate racial disparities in discipline, and to limit the role of police in schools.

We were breaking new ground here too. This was the first intergovernmental agreement where youth demanded to be involved in brokering the deal—and won. As a result, youth leaders from P&JU were asked to serve on President Obama's My Brother's Keeper task force. This put us in a position to explain and struggle for our viewpoint with federal decision makers, eventually influencing the federal guidelines on school discipline issued by the Obama administration in 2014.

We know that in order to truly create change, teachers, administrators, parents, and students have to be the ones to implement new discipline practices. So we collaborated with the Advancement Project, Denver Classroom Teachers Association, and the National Education Association on a project with the University of Denver and Denver Public Schools to create a training center for administrators, principals, teachers, and members of the community to learn how to implement restorative practices. This year we began training parents—the ones who fought for change—to lead restorative practices at two elementary schools.

We see the gains made in this work in the context of our quest for a society rooted in economic, social, and political equity—a world where humanity, justice, and equality are front and center in our decision making and policies. Self-determination, self-governance, and holding those in power accountable to the people are important components for realizing the democracy we all want and are trying to build. This is the spirit and vision that guides all of our work.

THE ROOTS OF CHICANO AND MEXICANO OPPRESSION IN THE US

We believe that the school-to-prison pipeline, a substandard education, and mass incarceration represent a continuation of historic efforts to maintain the subjugation, oppression, and colonization of people of color in the US.

P&JU believes that racism is an ideology that has been developed to support and justify the extreme exploitation and oppression of people of color. However, the minority are becoming the majority and driving a demand for change on many fronts.

But most of us do not understand the origins of the oppression of Chicanos and Mexicanos. Chicanos are people whose ancestors lived here when the Southwest was part of Mexico. During the bloody Mexican War of 1846–1848, the United States invaded the Southwest, which was a part of Mexico at the time; Mexico was able to push the US back to the tip of Texas. The people living in the Southwest Territory that the US stole in the war were colonized, lynched, and raped into submission. But they never gave up the struggle. Early on, Las Gorras Blancas and Joaquin Murrieta were inspirational freedom fighters; later the United Farm Workers Union and civil rights movement gave birth to the Chicano Movement and many revolutionary organizations. In the 1990s the government was forced to return a large piece of land in Colorado's San Luis Valley to families who had fought for many decades for their rights. The families won back their lands as well as their communal water, grazing, fishing, and timber rights.

People of color are becoming majority populations and have won significant gains. We are now seeing the right wing and the old-boy white networks resisting their loss of power. Donald Trump's presidential victory is pushing back on all the gains we have made. We need a more organized voice from the Chicano, Mexican, and black communities to address these issues and be a collective force in this country.

THE FREEDOM TO LEARN

To fight for educational equity and justice means we must end the school-to-jail track, stop the over-incarceration of people of color, and win the freedom to learn as a basic human right. In all of these struggles, we are striking back against the root causes of colonization, slavery, and genocide that follow people of color to this day. The more that elected officials, the police, and others attack, the more that people of color resist. There are thousands of students and communities fighting for immigrant rights and to support the "Dreamers"—young undocumented people who qualified for the Deferred Action for Childhood Arrivals or DACA program—to end the school-to-prison pipeline, and to stop police brutality and murder.

People are organizing to redistribute wealth by replacing police with counselors, moving public funds out of prisons and into communities, and using taxes to have free college education instead of increasing the wealth of the 1 percent.

In P&JU we fight for the basic human right to a quality education and life. And in all of this, people are organizing for their humanity, self-determination, and justice for as long as is needed to be free.

Our intergenerational model of organizing is powerful because it unites parents and youth. All parts of our communities play critical roles in the struggle. We recognize elders for their historical knowledge and the wisdom acquired through years of struggle. Young parents, especially mothers, are powerful and fight fiercely for their families and children. Youth are fearless and thirsty for change—and the world is theirs for the taking.

PART TWO

BROADENING THE MOVEMENT

Building Alliances for Systemic Change

6

◦—◦—◦—◦—◦—◦

#FIGHTFORDYETT

Fighting Back Against School Closings and the Journey for Justice

– Jitu Brown –

*Kenwood Oakland Community Organization,
Chicago, Illinois, and the Journey for Justice Alliance*

Jitu Brown discusses the mass closings of public schools in Chicago and other cities as a racist assault on black and brown communities. He tells the story of one community's refusal to accept the closing of their school, Walter Dyett High School, on the south side of Chicago. Committed parents led a hunger strike for thirty-four days, winning widespread support across the country, and ultimately saved the school. Jitu talks about how the local Fight for Dyett was "nationalized" as it galvanized the nascent Journey for Justice network into a nationwide alliance dedicated to militant opposition to the privatization of public education. He shows how multiracial coalitions rooted in the leadership of black and brown communities can build a powerful educational justice movement.

I WAS BORN AND RAISED on the South Side of Chicago. As a young adult, I lived in an apartment complex in the Bronzeville community, a historic center of African American culture. Bronzeville gave the world Mahalia Jackson, Richard Wright, Ida B. Wells, Harold Washington, Nat King Cole, Dinah Washington, Redd Foxx, and Dr. Daniel Hale Williams, to name a few.

But there was a lot of poverty and violence in my neighborhood too. As a young adult, I wanted to help the community, but I had become a rap artist and my music career began to take off. I was signed to Polygram Records and went on tour. When I came home, I had a promotional appearance at the William Shakespeare School, around the corner from my house. In talking to the students there about why positive hip-hop is important, one young man slouched in his chair and said, "You cool, man, but you not coming back." He was telling me that talk is cheap; we don't have anybody who is going to commit to stay and build with us. That really hit me. There was truth in what he was saying.

Soon after this, I met a community organizer. I told him the music industry felt like one big plantation and I was the product. He took me to the Kenwood Oakland Community Organization (KOCO), where I began volunteering in their youth programs. There came a moment when I could have either signed a solo deal with MCA Records or become an organizer. I chose the latter, and it was the best decision of my life.

Organizing was like a breath of fresh air. I saw people organizing to demand better housing, fight hunger, improve schools, and address issues facing youth and seniors. As I ran programs for KOCO, I learned how to organize through building deep relationships with people and meeting their basic needs. KOCO felt like home to me.

I began to see the lack of care and concern that the system has for black children. In my first education campaign, we tried to get the windows cleaned at the Albert Einstein School, which served children living in the Ida B. Wells housing project. The windows were so filthy that the school was dark. We had to fight for two whole years just to get clean windows for those children.

I became a local school council (LSC) member and began to work with other members on what they wanted to improve in their schools. We developed the LSC Institute, in which we trained a cadre of parents to become LSC facilitators. We won resources to take young people on college trips and arranged for parent meeting rooms at some of the schools in our neighborhood. We were beginning to make change, but we ran up against the city's plans for gentrification.

EDUCATION SABOTAGE

Bronzeville is ten minutes from downtown Chicago and right off the lakefront. It became a prime destination for gentrification. The district began to close schools in the Bronzeville community in the late 1990s. The closing of schools in Chicago coincided with the closing of many of the large public housing projects. As neighborhoods gentrified, the city eliminated traditional schools and opened alternatives that were attractive to the new gentrifiers.

In 2003 we obtained a copy of the Mid-South Plan, which called for the closure of twenty of the twenty-two schools in our neighborhood; they were going to be turned into contract schools, charter schools, or what they called "performance schools." We leaked this information to the *Chicago Tribune* and went to war with the district over the plan to shut down our schools.

We worked with SEIU (Service Employees International Union) Local 1, the Chicago Teachers Union, and Illinois ACORN (Association of Community Organizations for Reform Now), and together we stopped the Mid-South Plan. About nine months later, they came back with the citywide Renaissance 2010 plan calling for more school closings. We were shocked because there was so little regard for the voices of the parents in these schools who had just fought to stop their closing. There was no acknowledgment of the failure of the system to educate our children. Instead, the blame for so-called failing schools was placed on the children, the teachers, the parents, and community residents. We said, "No, our schools are not failing; *we've* been failed." Then we mobilized people to pressure elected officials to oppose the city's plan.

We lost on the first round of fighting Renaissance 2010. We ended up losing Doolittle West, which is now Urban Prep Charter School, and a number of other schools. Right away we began to see the impact of school closings up close. Suddenly we had 250 children from the closed school dumped into another school without so much as an additional special education teacher and no after-school resources. Teachers are used to having a few new students join their classroom each year; what do they do when over two dozen join? It's chaos.

We said, "This is not school reform; this is education sabotage. You're putting our children in conditions that you would not put your own children."

THE FIGHT FOR DYETT

I joined the local school council at Walter Dyett High School in 2003. There were no honors or Advanced Placement classes in the curriculum at the time. There were seven books in the library. We went to work at Dyett to introduce honors and AP classes and to create curriculum alignment between

Dyett's feeder elementary schools and the high school. We brought in a dynamic young principal.

In 2006, Chicago Public Schools CEO Arne Duncan closed Englewood High School and dumped about 125 of those children into Dyett with no resources. The school exploded. Fights broke out as young people from different gang neighborhoods were thrown together. It was a traumatic year, but we had to roll up our sleeves and figure it out. We believed in youth leadership, so we brought in Voices of Youth in Chicago Education, a youth organizing group that trained young people in how to organize their peers to improve their schools and communities. We did intense professional development, brought in mentorship programs, and implemented restorative justice.

We transformed an explosive school climate into a great school climate. Using student-led restorative justice and other innovative partnerships, Dyett doubled its graduation rate and increased its college-going rate by 41 percent in two years while decreasing discipline code violations by 85 percent.[1] In 2011 Dyett won the ESPN Rise Up Award, which came with a $4 million grant to upgrade our athletic facilities. We built a brand-new weight room and redid the gym floor. We had a state-of-the-art facility. Meanwhile, we had been working with parents at Dyett's feeder schools to articulate a vision for a pre-K through 12 system of education in our neighborhood, offering high-quality education from elementary to secondary school. Parents and young people were excited for the future.

The next year, in February 2012, the board of education voted to close Dyett High School. They decided to gradually phase out the school, which meant existing Dyett students started to lose their programs. It got to the point where students had to take art and physical education as online classes. For us, that was just deplorable.

One day two students, Diamond McCullough and Kesaundra Neal, came into my office and demanded to know what we were doing about the state of their school. They wanted to help, so they called a meeting and students came out in droves, packing the hall. That's how the Fight for Dyett began.

First we tried a federal civil rights complaint. Thirty-four Dyett students filed a Title VI complaint in 2013, arguing that since school closings were concentrated in black communities, the policy was racially discriminatory.

After several years of pressure from the complaint and our ongoing organizing, Chicago mayor Rahm Emanuel announced he would reopen Dyett as a charter school. But that wasn't what we wanted. We wanted an open-enrollment neighborhood school for all students.

We wrote a proposal to establish the Walter Dyett Global Leadership and Green Technology High School as the hub of a sustainable community schools village. Six feeder schools signed on. We developed this plan in the spirit of Ella Baker. It was an intentional grassroots democracy with all voices, including students, at the table. We enlisted national education experts to back our proposal. Despite our efforts, the district kept delaying the date for a decision about the fate of the school.

We escalated our organizing and raised the stakes. We chained ourselves to a statue outside of the mayor's office. We led 750 people in a march to his house. Dyett became a major news story in the city, but that still wasn't enough.

We decided to subject the mayor to national embarrassment. Twelve people, including myself, launched a hunger strike on August 17, 2015. That was the birthday of Marcus Garvey, one of the great leaders in black history. Garvey once said, "Look for me in the whirlwind, look for me in the storm. Look for me all around you, for my spirit will bring freedom to form." There was a torrential rainstorm the day we launched the hunger strike. The wind was so strong that it uprooted the tents and we had to chase them as they went flying down the street. Spiritually, that meant a lot to me: the ancestors supported our effort.

The Dyett campaign clearly showed that there are two Chicagos. When white parents on the north side express dissatisfaction, they have a meeting or two and their issue is addressed. When black parents on the South Side speak loud and clear, we're ignored or demonized.

On the twenty-fifth day of our hunger strike, Mayor Emanuel held a ribbon-cutting ceremony at predominantly white Lincoln Elementary School, near DePaul University on the north side. He gave them a $21 million annex while we starved in Washington Park. That told me all I needed to know.

The hunger strike raised a simple question for thousands of black people in this city: why can't our community have a say in what kind of school we want for our children?

One of the hard lessons that I learned from the hunger strike is that black people are not valued. This is not just about education. This is about a belief system that hates black people. This belief system infects every institution we deal with. It infects policing. It denies us educational opportunity on purpose. It's the same belief system that victimizes immigrant families. It's Donald Trump's belief system when he was a high-level slumlord who wouldn't rent apartments to black people.

This belief system has never been confronted within the white community and within America in general. The evil of sabotaging a child's education never comes up.

BREAKING THE MEDIA WHITEOUT

The Chicago media barely covered the first five or six days of the hunger strike. So we tapped our national networks for support: the Journey for Justice Alliance, the Alliance to Reclaim Our Schools, the American Federation of Teachers (AFT), and the Advancement Project. We flew in AFT president Randi Weingarten and featured high-profile elected officials like Chuy García in a press conference on the grounds of Dyett. That broke the media "whiteout," and our strike was everywhere.

We landed on the front page of the *New York Times* and had several articles about us in the *Washington Post*. Newspapers from Istanbul to Johannesburg ran stories about the hunger strike. #FightForDyett and other supportive hashtags trended strongly for four days with nearly one hundred thousand tweets during the month.[2] People from all over the world fasted with us. They would make a video or take a picture of themselves with a sign that said #FightForDyett; their video messages often went viral. It was impossible to minimize our effort as the pressure mounted locally, nationally, and internationally.

Finally the district offered to keep Dyett open as an arts academy. So after thirty-four days, we decided to end the hunger strike. We didn't win all that we wanted, but we succeeded in having Dyett reopen as a neighborhood school rather than a charter school. Although they made Dyett an art school instead of a school of global leadership and green technology, school officials assured us that they would implement a substantial portion of our curriculum. We believed that we had won and could work with the new plan to shape it the way we wanted.

Today Dyett is open and serving neighborhood children. There has been $16 million in new investments. Nearly all freshmen are on track to graduate. There's a great environment in the school. Dyett is going to be a sustainable community school. We have our curriculum team doing professional development for the Dyett teachers so that next year we can add sustainability to the curriculum.

The hunger strike was powerful because it resonated with people all over the world who feel disenfranchised and disrespected as human beings. The sacrifice of people going on a hunger strike touched people's hearts. When people heard that folks in a low-income black community wanted a school focused on global leadership and green technology, they were inspired. People identify Rahm Emanuel as part of the 1 percent, so this became the People Versus the 1 Percent. Black and brown folks understand that privatization feeds the 1 percent and is spreading like a plague everywhere in the world, from Chicago to Chile, and now other folks are starting to recognize this reactionary trend as well.

JOURNEY FOR JUSTICE

The Journey for Justice Alliance (J4J) played a critical role in nationalizing the Dyett hunger strike, by which I mean it helped bring national attention to a local fight in a way that catalyzes broader movements.

J4J operates in the spirit of Ella Baker and Septima Clark: we trust and believe in the brilliance of human beings, regardless of whether they're a PhD or a no D. How do you deal with a city that is racially toxic, where your life can be snuffed out at any moment? How do you keep your spirits up? For answers, I look no further than Mrs. Irene Robinson, a spirited grandmother of seventeen who we could not keep off the hunger strike. I have learned so much from her strength and core beliefs.

The idea for J4J came when I got a call from Zakiyah Ansari, a community organizer from the Alliance for Quality Education in New York City. She talked about how she felt alone, and I replied that I felt the same. We reached out to other like-minded people, such as the folks in the Baltimore Algebra Project, Youth United for Change, the Philadelphia Student Union, and the Alliance for Educational Justice. We asked, "What can we do about the privatization of public education?"

We decided to take a journey to Washington, DC. We marched on the US Department of Labor, because young people were concerned about summer jobs, and marched to the Department of Education to protest school privatization. We ended up mobilizing about two thousand people. It was powerful. Riding the high after that experience, we organized a community hearing at the Department of Education to pressure Secretary of Education Arne Duncan to support sustainable community schools. We eventually won some funds for those schools in the school improvement grants, and that was the beginning of J4J.

Alone in our local groups, we can't beat the highly organized infrastructure behind school privatization. That's like throwing rocks at tanks. We have to organize strong membership-based grassroots community organizations and link them together to win education equity in our time. Stopping school closings became a necessary part of our work, but our main priority is advancing community voices in public education.

J4J has developed an education platform with seven pillars: (1) a moratorium on school privatization, (2) the building of ten thousand sustainable community schools across the country, (3) an end to zero-tolerance discipline policies, (4) a halt to the attack on black teachers, (5) an end to privatization schemes that take away our democratic voice, (6) a stop to the over-testing of our youth, and (7) the use of multiple assessments to gauge our students' progress.

THE CANCER OF RACISM ON THE LEFT

The Left must deal with a cancer that exists within it: the deep seed of racism. There's an arrogance that says, "Racism doesn't apply to me; I'm progressive." Nothing could be further from the truth.

When I spoke to a group of organizers in Buffalo, they pushed back on what I was saying about racism. I asked, "How many of my white brothers and sisters grew up with decent schools in your community?" Most of them raised their hands. I continued, "How many of you had to get arrested or do sit-ins to get them?" They just stared blankly at me. "That's what the Left doesn't see," I told them.

The basic quality-of-life institutions that white Americans take for granted, such as schools and health clinics, are intentionally denied in black communities. You build a community by investing in those institutions; you destroy a community by denying those institutions. That is a reality of life for black people in cities all over this country. A trust has been betrayed. We want to be a part of the American Dream, but the hatred for us has never been reconciled.

The white Left is progressive until it comes to black and brown self-determination—that is, black and brown communities deciding for themselves what they need. Instead, too often in multiracial coalitions, black and brown people have to shrink in order to be accepted. We have to go along with the dominant majority and dilute our demands. As a result, we get reforms that are like a Band-Aid on a bullet wound; we don't get transformative change.

At J4J we organize black and brown families who are up in arms. We say, "If you want to work in brother- and sisterhood, don't ask me to shrink anymore. My child's life is just as important as yours. My children are just as beautiful, just as brilliant. I have the right to a clean place to live, just like you do. I have the right to have a grocery store and to own the businesses in my community, like you do."

The Fight for Dyett was a blueprint for building multiracial coalitions rooted in self-determination. The hunger strike was a militant, multiracial effort led by black people, who are the most impacted, and it was supported by a diverse coalition. We showed that unity rooted in self-determination builds a powerful movement that can win not only for black people but for everyone who is impacted by injustice.

We sometimes organize as if we're just trying to fight the good fight. Well, I ain't trying to fight the good fight. I'm trying to win.

7

--o--o--o--o--o--o--

THERE IS NO NATIONAL WITHOUT THE LOCAL

Grounding the School Discipline Movement in the Mississippi Delta

– Joyce Parker –

Citizens for a Better Greenville and
the Mississippi Delta Catalyst Roundtable

Joyce Parker talks about the efforts of the Mississippi Delta Catalyst Roundtable to challenge systemic racism in the Deep South. When zero tolerance became the new way to deny black people an education, black communities in Mississippi were some of the first to name the phenomenon of "schoolhouse to jailhouse." Joyce shows how small community organizations in rural areas can build the power to change systems when they link together across the Delta and to a national alliance like the Dignity in Schools Campaign. She also shows how the organizing work in the Delta helped ground the national campaign in the experiences of local black communities, concluding that there can be no strong national movement without deep local roots.

I COME FROM A LARGE FAMILY with a long history in the Mississippi Delta. My mother, who died at age ninety-seven, was raised by her grandmother, who was a slave until she turned twelve. My mom was a cook and my dad was a cab driver.

My parents sent their children to college. I received a degree in criminal justice and was hired as the first black female police officer in Greenville. But I faced discrimination as a black woman and was eventually forced out. My college degree opened other doors, reminding me of what my parents always said: "No one can take away from you the things that you know and have learned, the things in your head." I worked as a permanent substitute teacher, drove a school bus while working in the media resource department, and became a school attendance officer. I also worked as an alarm company operator, training young ladies who had good skills but had dropped out of school. All of these experiences led me to where I am now, a community organizer advocating for children and families.

SEPARATE BUT NOT EQUAL

As a child, I never thought of racism. Growing up in the black community, we had our side of town, and we had the best of the best, including our own movie theater. But one day at our family's weekly Sunday dinner, my brother said the city council was going to merge the white high school and the black high school. That's when we saw the disparities: the black high school didn't have a functioning science lab. Meanwhile, the white high school had just remodeled and added a math and science wing. We realized then that our schools were separate but not equal.

My brother had been exposed to the civil rights movement at Jackson State University. He knew of Hollis Watkins, one of the founders of Southern Echo, a nonprofit organization that provides training and technical assistance to black-led community organizations in the Delta. My brother and I reached out to Southern Echo in 2000. Echo had relationships at the Mississippi Department of Education, so the group helped us file a formal complaint about the disparity in the science labs, and the department came down to investigate. In the meantime, our school board decided to make $120,000 in renovations to the science lab in the predominantly black school. But the state education department said that the black high school needed $240,000, and the board agreed to pay. For those of us in this community who had never done anything like that before, it was a major win.

At the time, we didn't call this "organizing." It was just something that started at the family dinner table, addressing the needs of children. Through the training that we got from Southern Echo, our small community group became an organization, Citizens for a Better Greenville, with the purpose of addressing education issues. We started working with parents by forming a parent support group to discuss special education issues.

I learned early on in my conversations with parents that they could only connect to things within their experience. Parents did not understand that regardless of whether their children had special needs or were in general education, the system was the same: their children were losing out.

There was a major fight in one of our high schools during that time, and, as a result, students were about to be suspended. The school security officer knew the work of Citizens for a Better Greenville and called us to ask if we would work with the parents. We met with the parents and asked them what they wanted to do. They responded, "We did not send our children here to fight. We want to be in the building."

We helped parents form "Parents on Patrol." They went on patrol to ensure success for the students. We also began to develop our young people through a group called Youth as Public Speakers.

THE PREVENTION OF SCHOOLHOUSE TO JAILHOUSE

Our work with Southern Echo led us to make connections to organizing groups across the state of Mississippi. Hollis Watkins and Leroy and Helen Johnson with Southern Echo worked in some of the poorest communities in the country. Helen and her sister Ellen were seeing school-age black males just hanging out on the corner in Holmes County, where they lived. They asked one young man they saw every day what was he doing out on the street. He told them he had been suspended from school. Talking with more youth on the street, they heard that schools were suspending students for minor offenses, putting them out on the streets, and often referring them to juvenile courts. The parents began to see the connection between the schoolhouse and the jailhouse.

In the early 2000s the groups in the Southern Echo network started the Prevention of Schoolhouse to Jailhouse campaign. We brought together about forty state and national organizations—including the Southern Poverty Law Center, NAACP Legal Defense Fund, and Advancement Project—to talk about this issue.

Out of these meetings we formed the Mississippi Coalition for the Prevention of Schoolhouse to Jailhouse. We started a campaign to close some of the "training schools" that we had in Mississippi. "Training schools" is a misnomer. The schools weren't training people in anything. They were just prisons for children. They were incarcerating children and not doing anything to prepare them to come back to the community or back to school.

We pushed back very hard, because our children were being arrested for status offenses, noncriminal behaviors that are only applied to minors, such as running away or being "incorrigible" or defiant. If they were adults, these would not have even been crimes.

Children were taken out of our schools and communities and put in settings where girls were sexually abused. One child said he was served breakfast with a big roach on it. And the medical attention was substandard. Reports about frequent mistreatment of young people, such as beatings and solitary confinement, led to a federal investigation.

We created maps showing that the communities that lacked resources and had failing schools were the same communities with a high proportion of students being arrested or disciplined. The maps also showed that the state was locating prisons in communities with the lowest third-grade reading scores.

We shared our findings with Congressman Bennie Thompson, who then started a campaign based on this issue in Mississippi. Our efforts and the pressure of a federal investigation got the state to close the notorious Columbia Training School for Girls. Working through the coalition, we also won passage of the Juvenile Justice Reform Acts of 2004 and 2005, designed to eliminate the abuse of incarcerated children, to guarantee their right to education, and to create community-based alternatives to incarceration. These were some of our first victories.

WEAVING A NETWORK

A hallmark of Southern Echo's approach to organizing is to link local organizations like Citizens for a Better Greenville into statewide networks that address the collective needs of communities. We formed the Mississippi Delta Catalyst Roundtable to coordinate the work of our local groups on educational justice issues.

Around 2007, we heard about a newly forming national coalition to combat the school-to-prison pipeline, the Dignity in Schools Campaign (DSC). They were looking at human rights and using a framework like ours around how children were being treated in schools. If they were framing the national conversation on this issue, we wanted to be a part of it. I became a leader of DSC nationally, and local groups in the roundtable joined DSC as members too. We participated in DSC's National Week of Action, bringing greater attention to our work. We sent delegations to Washington, DC, for DSC's Days on the Capitol, where local members lobbied their congressional representatives from across the country.

Being part of the Mississippi Delta Catalyst Roundtable and DSC and joining with other regional, state, and national organizations helped Citizens for a Better Greenville build its capacity. It also built collective power, in terms of having more voices than just a single organization. Now we have 10 organizations in this region working together and reaching out nationally to the 120 other organizational members in DSC. Building a network helped us avoid reinventing the wheel. Southern Echo's relationship with the Mississippi Department of Education took years to build. But in just a few weeks we could tap those relationships to advance our work.

As new members and leaders joined the roundtable, I made a personal commitment to do for them what Helen and Ellen Johnson had done for me. I would look around the room and ask myself, What do these new and emerging organizations need to get their work done? I began calling myself a "network weaver," building relationships and connecting local leaders from organizations across the Delta.

Much of the work we have done through the Mississippi Delta Catalyst Roundtable has had a state focus. We became a part of the Special Education Advisory Council at the state level. We became advocates for state legislation that would benefit our community. We provided information locally about what was happening in the state legislature to make sure we had informed communities. We became the community's voice in conversations when our legislators had questions about how various bills would impact our communities.

One of our major accomplishments at the state level was helping to win passage of the Mississippi Adequate Education Program (MAEP) and ensuring that the state fully funded it. In 2007 we convinced the legislature to increase funding to public education by $650 million, an enormous amount considering the abysmally low funding levels in rural communities in the Delta. Up until that point, Mississippi was funding only a third-grade education. Even now, with the passage of that law, it funds only an eighth-grade education, but that is a major improvement. Getting the MAEP passed and funded was probably our most significant victory.

THE MISSISSIPPI MODEL

Mississippi is usually on the bottom of everything. That is one reason why our work on the school-to-prison pipeline has been noteworthy: we have been out in front in this work. We were one of the very first places to recognize the connection of schoolhouse to jailhouse and address it. I made it very clear that in order for our network to participate in DSC, we would not lead from behind. We had to be a part of the decision-making structure and the leadership. We brought our organizing experiences and stories from our communities.

In the end the structure of DSC mirrors what we did in Mississippi, where the state coalitions like the roundtable helped build the capacity of local groups. We insisted that the national network had to support the work of local communities, not just take all the resources for itself and focus on Washington.

There is no national campaign without local impact. Local communities need to know that the efforts are about them rather than people telling them what to do. The local communities tell the campaign what they need done. That approach has been at the core of the success of the Dignity in Schools Campaign. Before this, national groups would fly in and work on something with the local groups; then they would fly back out, write up a report, and get all the money. The local organizations didn't get anything. We didn't even get support from the national groups anymore.

When I came into DSC, they were working on their model school discipline code of conduct. The roundtable had just completed a community process addressing the development of our code of conduct, so I brought our experience into the DSC process. I told DSC that we needed to take this model code into communities and let people dissect it and add to it. In this way it would be an authentic document that came from families, parents, and students. For DSC the relationships that came with the model code were as important as the code itself. In the end a young man from Southern Echo, Greg Johnson, collected all the input and made the code a living document.

BRINGING THE NATIONAL TO THE LOCAL

We used the model code with our own Greenville district. At the time, our district had a zero-tolerance policy. That meant children could be suspended for anything at the discretion of the principal. We used our grassroots approach to work with the Advancement Project, a national civil rights advocacy organization that was looking at discipline data across the country. The Greenville School District was listed as one of the top three in the country when it came to discipline disparities for black males. The Advancement Project recommended that the district adopt the matrix that Baltimore City Schools had developed in its code of conduct. The matrix presents a comprehensive list of student behavior expectations, establishing appropriate school responses for violations. This matrix was probably the most progressive model in the country at the time for guiding educators away from punitive discipline and toward positive and supportive approaches. The matrix was aligned with our own proposals in our model code, so we supported it. The district agreed to use this matrix, and that was a big win for us, ending zero tolerance in our district.

Sometimes you are not welcome in your own home. Our relationship with the Advancement Project and with other national organizations made it much easier for us to be involved and to be recognized in a different way. Our superintendent built a relationship with us, and we have been able to influence policies, practices, and procedures here in our school district. When the data came out two years later, it showed that we had significantly reduced the number of suspensions in our schools. In other words, our national connections increased our power and influence locally.

Another result of this work was that the superintendent established a Supportive Services Department to provide wraparound services. This meant that counselors, social workers, nurses, dropout-prevention strategists, and parent engagement specialists all work together, focusing on why children are failing academically and behaviorally. They take a supportive approach instead of imposing punitive measures.

As we called attention to the schoolhouse-to-jailhouse pipeline, we wanted to explore alternatives to locking up children. A new national campaign called the Juvenile Detention Alternative Initiatives (JDAI) selected Greenville and surrounding Washington County as sites for its program. Our organization became one of the co-facilitators. JDAI brings together the

Department of Human Services, churches, mental health agencies, schools, and anybody in the community who works with children. The result is that many of our students who commit status offenses are no longer placed in jail. Our latest report showed that, since JDAI started, the number of students in the detention center declined by over a third.

The behavior we see in school should not be dealt with in a punitive manner. Trauma-informed care is crucial. We must address the trauma that our children experience, such as when a child has been up all night with parents who are fighting, or children who are being sexually assaulted. Each situation should be dealt with in a supportive manner, where we are repairing harm and restoring the children.

As organizers, we are the connectors. The school was saying that the Department of Human Services didn't work with them, and the department and the courts were saying the schools didn't work with them either. We stand in the middle and say, "This is about our children, and you need to work together." Then we hold others accountable—not in a way that creates animosity or adversarial relationships, but in a supportive manner, helping them to work with each other.

In 2014 the mayor of Greenville, who was white and had grown up in this community, said on national TV that the schools in Greenville were not good enough for his children. That was a slap in the face to our community. But the same mayor accepted President Obama's challenge for My Brother's Keeper, in which leaders commit to investing in young black and brown men and boys. For us in Mississippi, we connect that directly to this notion that prisons are located based on third-grade reading scores: the lower the scores, the more prisons.

When the mayor pledged to be part of My Brother's Keeper, he asked one of our sister organizations, the Delta Foundation, to coordinate, and they invited us to co-facilitate with them. Our first initiative was to make sure that every child was ready for school by first grade. The second was that all third-grade children should be able to read at grade level. And the third initiative talked about children being able to complete high school.

Our superintendent told us that a quarter of the students who come into first grade in Greenville have not been in a learning environment before they arrive. He was able to budget for a stand-alone pre-K school. We also were able to collaborate with Head Start and arrange for them to provide training with our school district for the child-care providers in the district. Our child-care providers are now able to go into our schools and see what the curriculum looks like so that they can directly align their curriculum with that of the schools. Our school district can make sure that all providers are working together to help our children be ready to learn in first grade.

MY INSPIRATION

I don't have any children, but I thank God that he has placed so many children in my life. When my father passed away, there were 121 offspring listed in his obituary. When President Obama was reelected, my mom, the granddaughter of a slave, had five generations in the room with her watching a black president be named.

The only thing I ask of any parent who wants to stand up for their children is that if we work for your child, then you've got to help us to work for others. Whatever the change is, it must be systemic, so that even the parents or children we never see are taken care of.

I feel hopeful. I feel inspired. I feel very capable. And I feel honored to believe that God has me where he wants me to be. This job is really a ministry for me.

The most important thing for black people since integration is that we must go back to doing for ourselves and developing the skills and the tools that we innately have. We have to dig deep into our own communities and into our own selves and bring back the culture and understanding that we are valued. We've got to revive much of what we lost when we came to this country.

The next part of our work will be about cultural restoration for our young people, and even for us as adults. We lost our culture coming over here, but you don't lose what's already in you. We've got to revive it and restore it.

8

THE SCHOOL IS THE HEART
OF THE COMMUNITY

Building Community Schools
Across New York City

– Natasha Capers –

Coalition for Educational Justice, New York City

Natasha Capers describes the vital role public schools play in the life of a community. Becoming a parent organizer, she helped the Coalition for Educational Justice place parent and community organizing at the center of the community schools movement in New York City. Community schools provide health and social services, but they can do more; they serve as hubs for deep collaboration between parents, educators, and organized communities that transform teaching and learning. Through the PS 2013 campaign, the coalition won Mayor Bill de Blasio's support to fund over 130 community schools across New York City. Natasha shows that, if done well, community schools can become a model for public schools that support and empower low-income children of color.

WHEN MY CHILDREN WERE still in elementary school in New York City, Mayor Michael Bloomberg released his annual list of schools that were "low performing" and slated for closure. My children's school, PS 298 in Brownsville, Brooklyn, was on the list.

PS 298 is my alma mater. I attended that school until sixth grade. It's surrounded by New York City public housing, but it was always considered a jewel of Brownsville. It had great programming, with a glee club, athletics, and a newspaper. And this was just an elementary school.

I was a "mathlete" at the school. We had opportunities to get out of the building and do things and explore. But over the years, the school declined. When my children began attending, I could see that there had been disinvestment. At one point the school didn't have a functioning library or a librarian. There wasn't an up-to-date computer lab. Many of the after-school programs had been cut. And yet I loved and still love PS 298; I see the glory that is within the walls of my alma mater.

I was the vice president of the parent association and chair of the school leadership team at the time the school was slated for closure in the fall of 2011. I received a call from Fiorella Guevara from the Annenberg Institute for School Reform, who was working with the Coalition for Educational Justice (CEJ), to organize parents at schools that were on the closure list to try to save their schools. CEJ is a collective that works toward creating educational equity in the system at the citywide level. I joined the fight because I had a historical understanding of where my school had been and the wonderful things that were possible there.

THE SCHOOL IS THE HEART OF THE COMMUNITY

School closure is devastating. The school is the heart of the community. Everything dear to me either happened in PS 298 or happened because of that school. I was able to go to college and pay for part of it through a music scholarship because I started singing in the third grade in the glee club. When people are flippant about closing a school, it wounds me. I think about who I might not have been if I hadn't been able to sing in that glee club. The school gives young people a foundation.

When a school is slated for closure, no one asks the really hard questions: Why aren't students achieving? What will it take for them to achieve? And what are the "experts" doing wrong? All the blame falls on all the wrong people. It's "the kids don't care, the parents don't care, and even the teachers don't care"—and none of that is true, nor is it the true source of any of the problems. Often when a school closes, another one opens in the same building with the same students, and the same horrible things just keep occurring.

We began to organize other parents to save the school. Fiorella and CEJ helped me understand that school closure was a deeper, citywide, and even statewide issue. She helped me to articulate an alternative vision for what could be possible for our school. I vowed that I would make PS 298 a community school if it's the last thing I do.

By organizing, we saved the school, and after the election of Mayor Bill de Blasio, PS 298 became a community school through New York City's Renewal School Program. The city's Department of Education started the program to transform low-performing schools into community schools with extended school days, mental health services, support from and for families, and extensive partnerships with community organizations. I was over the moon about it.

PS 298 is now doing great and has the resources it should have had all along. The school has been able to improve attendance and raise student proficiency rates. The principal has created an environment where students are excited about being in school. PS 298 is now much more like the school I attended as a child.

MEETING THE NEEDS OF THE WHOLE CHILD

After saving PS 298, I continued working with the Coalition for Educational Justice and became a leader with their statewide partner, the Alliance for Quality Education. Then I was hired as the CEJ coordinator.

CEJ is the largest parent-led group in New York City and comprises community-based organizations across all five boroughs that organize parents in black, brown, and immigrant communities. For example, the Queens parent committee of Make the Road New York advocates for school construction, because their schools are so overcrowded that many students have to take classes in temporary trailers. These groups push for change in an individual school or district, but there's only so much that a district superintendent or school principal can do without systemic change, especially in a system with more than seventeen hundred schools and mayoral control.

At CEJ we envision community schools as a hub for services that address the needs of the community at large, but specifically the needs of the student and family population at the school. Where there's a need for a dental clinic, mental health services, a food pantry, or laundry services, those things are made available to families.

We believe that by taking care of the needs of students and families, students will be more successful in schools; their test scores, grades, and attendance will all improve. For example, if you give a student a pair of glasses, they see better and they perform better academically. Similarly, if students are not hungry, they can focus better in class. Then we took it to the next level: if you can do all those things while also dissecting teaching and learning and improving everyday practices in the classroom, you will get the long-term systemic change that children need.

STRONG PARENT ENGAGEMENT

We want parents to be full partners in community schools. We see a relationship between intentional, strong parent engagement and what happens in the classroom. We brought the Academic Parent-Teacher Teams model into NYC schools with the help of the educational nonprofit WestEd. These teams hold parent-teacher conferences in a new and dynamic way. Schools traditionally conduct fifteen-minute parent-teacher conferences with individual families. In the new model, a teacher brings together *all* parents into the classroom, and together they look at achievement data and discuss the key skills that students need before advancing to the next grade.

All the parents work with the teacher to set both classroom and individual goals for their children. For example, the teacher may say, "We are working on growing the class's vocabulary by two hundred words, and this is how we're going to do it together as a team." The teacher and parents figure out how to work together to achieve the goal, and the teacher identifies resources, games, and activities that parents can use at home to help their children. At these meetings, parents have an opportunity to build a stronger relationship with the teacher and also with each other. The last Academic Parent-Teacher Team meeting of the school year discusses how to set students up for success in the following year by coming up with ways to sustain learning through the summer vacation.

How do you build strong relationships between the community and the school? How do you begin to shift how teachers view parents, how parents view teachers, and how each of them views young people? How do you grow the relationship academically? With our approach, the school asks parents to perform a teaching skill to reinforce academic practice and gives them the tools and support to be able to do that. Now you have a whole classroom full of parents who are immersed in learning and teaching practice. It is no longer just a one-sided equation; you have begun to equalize the relationship.

COMMUNITY SCHOOLS

What's different about a community school? When you walk in the door, you may first notice that there are a lot more resources and more hands on deck. A community school director coordinates the after-school programs, the medical clinics, and other services. This role allows principals to focus on being instructional leaders and allows the director to take on more of the social-emotional and support work.

You may see more parents in the building, because there are more workshops in such areas as English as a second language or Spanish as a second language, depending on what parents communicate that they want or need. Community schools provide an extra hour of instruction to students and offer a variety of after-school programs.

At their best, community schools feel more vibrant. The adults are happy to be there, so the students are happy to be there. Students report that it's more fun to be in their school. I have found that when a school lacks vibrancy, or where the adults aren't invested, it bleeds over to the students. At a community school, teachers and other adults have a renewed sense of excitement about being in the building.

SCHOOLS THAT REFLECT THE COMMUNITY

The teaching force in New York City is over 60 percent white, while 85 percent of students are children of color.[1] Students across the city and even across the country don't see themselves reflected in their teachers, nor do they see themselves reflected in the books they read.

Parents of color, especially immigrant families, are viewed as not caring about their children. I have seen Spanish-speaking families flat-out ignored. The school considers it a bother to find someone who speaks their language, so non-English-speaking parents cannot have a robust conversation about their children's academic performance.

The white-supremacist belief system that devalues communities of color is responsible for what is happening in schools and in communities that have seen complete disinvestment. For decades, no one cared about schools in Brownsville, Brooklyn; they ignored and underfunded them. Without a strong challenge, this belief system continues to be reinforced, even in community schools. We work extremely hard to shift how teachers and school staff view families so that they treat them as assets. We work to shift deficit thinking to asset-based thinking, and we help educators learn to listen to parents and hear what they are saying.

Another parent engagement model that we have brought to New York City is the Parent Teacher Home Visit. Teachers go through training, and then they call the family to set up a visit. The meeting can take place anywhere other than the school, such as in the neighborhood library. Teachers and staff need to know the communities where they are working. They can get to know families on a whole different level when they are not on the teacher's turf.

Teachers might ask, "Tell me about yourself. Tell me about your child. What are your hopes and dreams? What do you want them to get out of this year?" Teachers learn about the family and student as people, something they would not have been able to do if the conversations were solely about test scores.

Families immediately feel more comfortable with those teachers. Parents say, "I actually know someone at this school. If something happens, I have someone I can talk to." Home visits create new kinds of connections between schools, families, and communities.

ELECTORAL POWER

In 2013 CEJ launched a campaign to make improving public education a key issue in New York City's mayoral race. How do we shift away from the punitive school-closure model and toward infusing resources and support into struggling schools? We wanted to steer candidates toward community schools as a solution.

We took a good-guy/bad-guy approach—or, as I like to say, it was like a Labrador retriever and a pit bull. The Labrador is sweet, and you want to build a good relationship with her. The pit bull is the opposite.

The bad guy, or pit bull, was New Yorkers for Great Public Schools. NYGPS created wedge issues in public education to move candidates as far away as possible from Mayor Michael Bloomberg's policies of school closures, charter schools, and disinvestment. The closer you were to supporting the damaging things he did, the worse it seemed for you. NYGPS held continuous press conferences to keep the wedge issue in the news, to elevate public education as one of the top voter issues in the city.

The Labrador was "PS 2013," our campaign to uplift positive policy solutions. The coalition operated an online policy hub that talked in depth about changing outcomes for students of color. It featured the best things to do for students with special needs and promoted community schools. Contributors created policy papers that were just two or three pages long, making them accessible to a cross-section of readers.

We also ran a citywide charrette, or intensive planning process, which involved more than seventy-five community meetings with parents, students, community members, teachers, principals, and superintendents around the city. We asked questions like "What would you like to see in your ideal school?" and "What are the things you would want the next mayor to do for public education?" These were simple but direct questions that helped identify what people wanted to see happen. It is amazing how simple the questions are, yet they are often never asked.

Community members wanted art, music, and better physical education. They wanted more robust community services and better school food. These are all core tenets of community schools.

We then took the top twenty things that people wanted to see in their schools, and we created an installation in a bright blue bus that traveled around the city, providing an attractive container for all these ideas. Each idea had a different basket, and people would walk through the bus with a packet of tokens and vote for what they wanted to see in their schools. It was a way of engaging folks in a democratic process that is very much missing with public education in New York, because we have mayoral control instead of elected community school boards or local governance.

With the help of a design team of policy experts, we put out a road map for the next mayor that highlighted all the top ideas, including community schools. All the major candidates came to the mayoral forum at which we presented our platform. Throughout this time, parents from CEJ had been meeting with elected officials and with candidates to raise our issues. CEJ cannot endorse candidates, but we have the power to meet with folks and put before them a platform supporting community schools.

Because of all the talk and energy behind our campaign, candidates started to endorse community schools as an important strategy. Mayoral candidate Bill de Blasio pledged to open 100 community schools in his first term. De Blasio won the 2013 mayor's race, and by the end of his first full school year he transformed 130 schools into community schools; since then he has added nearly 100 more.

VICTORY

The fact that parents were so pivotal at bringing the community school model to New York City was a huge victory. These are black, brown, and immigrant families, and some of the leaders are monolingual Spanish speakers. We are not the usual folks who influence mayoral candidates. Our ability to influence the mayoral race in such a pivotal way speaks volumes to the impact of community organizing and to our vision for community schools.

Mayor Bill de Blasio's victory did not mean we could just walk away. After calling for 130 community schools, we began to support the transition of traditional schools to the new model, implement new parent-teacher relationships, and improve the quality of the instruction in those schools, among other initiatives.

We recently shifted our attention to another part of our community school platform: culturally responsive education. Now is the time for school communities to go deeper and shift their curricula to better represent and engage the history and culture of the students of color they serve.

LESSONS FOR ACTIVISTS

Getting someone to say they will create community schools is the easy part. The hard part is this: after they say yes, then what?

There are three lessons to take away from our community school campaign in New York. The first lesson is that even when you have a friendly administration that is seemingly giving you what you want, the work doesn't stop. It shifts and changes and gets harder. Never let up.

The second lesson is to be thoughtful and mindful about the type of schools and the number of schools your organization can support. New York has more than 1,700 schools, so even the current total of 225 community schools does not seem like a lot. But that actually is a lot of schools to have taken on all at once; in fact, it is the largest school improvement plan in the country. And because these were some of the schools that struggled most in the city, we were asking a lot of them. In hindsight, I think creating smaller cohorts and building a bit more slowly would have worked better. Our children cannot wait, but they also deserve strong improvements that will work.

The third lesson is that planning is critical. I think we should have pushed for implementation to start after a planning year. The schools had little knowledge about how to transition to the new model, community-based organizations did not always know the best ways to support the schools, and there was no real training for community school resource directors. There needed to be a strong planning year when staff could learn their roles before diving into the deep end. Better preparation increases the likelihood of success.

A bonus lesson is that you must have your own definition of success. If you leave it up to your critics, they will never say you're successful. If you leave it up to test scores, those scores will not tell the full story. Start by figuring out in year one what success means. How does that shift in year two, and year three, and year four? What are all the measures of success that matter beyond test scores?

We must make community schools high quality, always raising the bar. Those are our babies, nieces, nephews, and our neighbors' children in those classrooms. We want to make them the best that they can be.

9

----o-o-o-o-o----

FIGHTING FOR TEACHERS, CHILDREN, AND THEIR PARENTS

Building a Social Justice Teachers' Union

– Brandon Johnson –

Chicago Teachers Union

Brandon Johnson tells the story of the transformation of the Chicago Teachers Union from a traditional "wages and hours" union to a social justice union working with families and communities of color for racial equity and justice. As an African American middle school teacher, Brandon saw the devastating impact of school closures on black and brown communities. In response to attacks on public education, the union launched a bold and historic strike. The strike showed how teachers can unite with parents and community organizations to build a powerful educational justice movement that works to protect teachers, improve the quality of education for all students, and challenge the profound inequities that children face where they live and learn.

THE MOMENT YOU SIGN UP to become a teacher in the Chicago public school system you become an advocate, because you're always searching for opportunities to meet the needs of your students. The system often falls short— from classroom materials, to reading and math support, to social and emotional development. Most schools don't have social workers and counselors, for example, even though there is an overwhelming need for them.

While I was teaching at Jenner Academy, a K–8 school near the Cabrini-Green housing projects, I saw many policies that resulted in tremendous destabilization. For example, the district closed a neighborhood school located on the other side of the boundary in gang territory. Those students had to walk across gang lines every day to attend their new elementary school. As our students left the building, gangs of students gathered outside, waiting to confront them and make it impossible for them to get back home. It was chaotic. A local police commander told me that he deployed more police officers at this elementary school than at all the high schools in the area combined. My role as an educator extended well beyond teaching time, because we had to ensure that students could walk safely across the street.

We faced tremendous stress every day. Somehow, despite these extreme circumstances, students were expected to learn and teachers were expected to teach; the political leadership had no regard for those black lives. That's when I started to realize that we needed a teachers' union that would understand the broader fight beyond wages and benefits.

After teaching at Jenner Academy for several years, I reluctantly left to teach at Westinghouse High School on the west side, close to my home. Karen Lewis had just been elected president of the Chicago Teachers Union (CTU). The new leadership was looking to make some dynamic changes by adopting an organizing model instead of the service model that it had followed for too long. I joined the organizing summer institute, where I had the experience of talking to our members about what a good school system could look like. I spent six weeks of a hot summer knocking on hundreds of doors across the city. At the end of the summer, the union leadership asked me to join the staff and help prepare for what became the 2012 Chicago teachers strike.

Over that summer of door knocking, I learned that my experiences at Jenner were not unique. The city was disinvesting in schools in black neighborhoods across the city. As students lost their school, the children of gentrifiers occupied it. They would close a predominantly black school, forcing the students to cross gang territory, and open an overwhelmingly white selective enrollment school in the building. It made me sick: this intentional policy to remove people who were indigenous to the community to make room for the new Chicagoans.

A CONSCIOUS BLACK EDUCATOR

There is a tremendous need for conscious black men to teach in Chicago schools. To be honest, the challenge has often felt overwhelming. I'm not magical. Black children do not automatically listen to me more because I'm a black man. But seeing a black man working full-time as a professional in their schools can have a tremendous impact on children.

Conscious teachers recognize that the way to educate children is by giving them the opportunity to ask questions and not simply follow directions. They engage with students, learning about their experiences and ideas and hopes. I do not teach a story and just say, "Answer these five questions." I also have to be aware that the conditions in which the students live are real political problems. For example, one day a student in my classroom had his head down for a long time, and I thought something might be wrong. I said, "What's going on, man? You've had your head down for forty minutes."

"No, Mr. Johnson, I'm for real," he replied. "I'm not feeling well." He opened his mouth, and I saw that one of his teeth had a hole from severe decay. There was no nurse in the building that day. That hole had not opened up just the previous night. This had been a condition he'd had for some time. These are political problems.

I want to help my students think critically about their environment. I want them to understand why they have an untreated medical problem and why there's no nurse in their school. Maybe then, if our union and community allies are successful, when students come to school with a medical condition, there will be a nurse to treat them.

THE MAKINGS OF A SOCIAL JUSTICE UNION

You do not win elections during the voting. You win in the buildup.

Back in the 1990s, when school closures, consolidations, and charter expansions began, the old CTU leadership did not put up a fight. When they announced that the last school was going to close in Cabrini and that the school where I was teaching would be the receiving school for all the displaced students, the union leadership focused only on how to keep as many jobs as possible. Local teachers were left to speak out against the closure on their own. There was no fight about all the social and economic injustices that occurred because of school closures.

Teachers who were part of the Caucus of Rank and File Educators, led by Karen Lewis, began to organize protests and rallies against mass teacher layoffs and budget cuts. I said to my colleagues, "This is what a union needs to look like."

The caucus won the election for the union leadership in 2010, and Karen Lewis became the new president of the CTU. We moved quickly to reorient ourselves as a social justice union. We look at social justice in terms of equity and how schools are resourced, but we also look at it from a racial and economic justice point of view. The school "deformers," as we refer to the so-called reformers, have caused tremendous harm. Low-income black communities have suffered the most under these privatization schemes.

For example, North Lawndale, on the west side of Chicago, has a profound history. Dr. Martin Luther King stayed in North Lawndale when he came to Chicago. This historic neighborhood has just been devastated by an unemployment rate that resembles that of the Great Depression, and from sustained disinvestment in housing and schools. Many schools in North Lawndale, like 140 schools across Chicago, have no librarians. Schools often have no social workers, counselors, or nurses, and offer physical education as an online course. In addition, many schools lack proper ventilation, so they are either boiling hot or freezing cold. Instead of investing in these schools to build up the community, Mayor Rahm Emmanuel and his handpicked school board implements a so-called turnaround school policy with which they fire every person in the building, including the cafeteria workers. They bring in a whole new set of teachers who are young and white, and most of them don't stay longer than eighteen months. The turnover is far worse than in a traditional neighborhood school, and the problems continue.

This was and is an injustice. We knew the union had to fight for schools that all children deserve. To gain credibility beyond securing wages and benefits, we had to connect our working conditions to our students' learning conditions. Moreover, we had to fight to improve both the quality of the learning environment and the quality of the living conditions that our students, their families, and our members endure every day.

TEACHERS AND COMMUNITY UNITED
We moved to shift our teachers away from the service model of unionism—in which a teacher has an issue and the union representative meets with the principal to resolve it—to seeing themselves as a powerful force to protect members and students in their own building. Members must recognize that

the union is only as strong as its membership. Teachers have to organize in their building against attacks on the contract but also against violations of students' rights, such as the right to Individualized Education Program accommodations for special education students. That involves organizing parents as well.

Historically, there have been divisions between teachers' unions and parents of color. We addressed this up front by creating a community table called the Grassroots Education Movement (GEM). Parent and community organizations sit at this table as partners with the union. Their views matter to us and helped shape our new program. The CTU program calls for fully funding education; reducing class sizes; improving facilities; challenging inequities in resources and school discipline; providing wraparound services with more counselors and nurses; adding classes in art, music, and physical education; and partnering with parents in all we do.

Our community partners have led us in actions that have pushed our union's comfort zone. For example, they advocated for GEM to organize a march to Mayor Emanuel's house in 2011 to protest his plan for further privatization of public education. The mayor was at the height of his popularity, with a 70 percent approval rating, and we were hesitant. Our community and parent organizations insisted we had to take it right to the mayor's front door—and they meant it literally. They said, "We need to march in his neighborhood and tell the mayor that this is harming us. We can't find you downtown, so we're going to find you at your home." Our community partners challenged the union and our membership, insisting that we be far more confrontational, and they were right. It was a dynamic action that energized our members and showed where we stood as a union. This is the important thing about organizing and fighting for an educational justice movement: you must be prepared to not just talk about what you want but to take some risk as well.

We worked with our members to understand that you can't fight for black children without fighting for their black parents. Teachers need to build relationships with parents of the children they serve. If parents and teachers are not collaborating to bring about a better working and learning environment, we don't have a fighting chance at beating back those who are undermining public education. In fact, had it not been for parents working alongside our membership with their children, we certainly would not be the force we are for educational justice.

Prior to the strike, CTU members spent countless hours talking with parents in our buildings. We knocked on thousands of doors across the city. Many teachers and parent allies led discussions at their churches. We talked to folks about what a school system should look like, not just about our pay. We would ask, "What do you want from your schools?" Parents would tell us what they wanted but would also say, "You all deserve to get paid too." They recognized the hard work that we put in. We agreed that you can fight for a good school and protect the dignity of those who work there. Those conversations laid the foundation for widespread parent and community support for our strike.

STRIKE!

In 2012 the CTU went on strike for the first time in twenty-five years. We prepared our members to take this step by, first, making the case that we could better protect our profession by defending public education and our children. Second, we put forward a real plan for what schools needed to look like, and we effectively identified those people, including the mayor, who stood in the way. Finally, we began to raise awareness of the inequities that many people said couldn't be fixed but we refused to accept. As a result, our members realized that we needed to withhold our labor in order to beat back the mayor's proposal that would hurt both teachers and students. The mayor proposed high-stakes evaluations for teachers, cuts to benefits, and removal of the cap on class sizes, and he refused to respond to our demands for a more well-rounded education for students.

The 2012 strike became about, How do you make sure that the dignity of teaching—our humanity as educators, paraprofessionals, clerks, nurses, and social workers—is respected? How do we make this fight for education about what people ultimately deserve? And, finally, who should pay for it?

A key to our success was winning parents to our side. Parents and community groups joined us on picket lines, and polls showed that a majority of parents supported our demands. This was unprecedented. Meanwhile, people forget that CTU members are also parents of children in the public schools in Chicago. I myself live in Austin, on the west side of Chicago, which has been deemed the most violent neighborhood in Chicago. We were overwhelmed by the support of parents, and we are still humbled by the continued support and the belief that parents have in our work.

The strike was a success. We stopped merit pay, protected benefits and retirement security, saved the cap on class sizes, and pushed the board to offer greater variety in subjects for students, including expanded access to art, music, and physical education.

The strike had a big political impact beyond the contract. The larger success was to bring community and labor together to fight for public schools and the rights of workers. Our strike inspired teachers to go on strike in other school districts in Illinois, even in some of the more affluent areas. The strike led to stricter accountability for charter expansion. It also led to teachers organizing in charter schools. Meanwhile, bus operators and train operators prepared to take strike votes too. We elected progressive members to the city council as a result of the 2012 strike.

The strike also expanded democracy. The state legislature passed a law to make the school board an elected body, ending mayoral control, although the governor failed to sign it. Funding education has become a priority in the state by calling for the rich to pay their fair share in taxes.

You cannot fix twenty-five years of bad policy in one contract. You must continue to fight. That's why we led a one-day strike on April 1, 2015, that shut down the entire city. It included university professors and activists from Black Lives Matter, bus drivers, and train operators. In 2012 we showed it was possible to wage a fight and win. People recognized that you can actually build a movement and fight back against corporate greed and politicians who are protecting the interests of the 1 percent.

AN ATTACK ON BLACK LABOR

As I recall, Dr. King said that the enemies of the Negro are the enemies of labor. That speaks to me and explains why I work for the CTU. If advocates for civil rights and labor rights were to ever work together, what enormous potential we would have.

When you look at the attack on public education, it's not just an attack on the right to public accommodations. It's also an attack on black labor. In 1995, when a Republican-led Illinois General Assembly and governor turned control of the Chicago Public Schools over to the mayor, half of the teaching force was black. Now that percentage is down to 22 percent, and we are seeing this kind of decline across the country.

The attack on labor, through school privatization and closures, has decimated the black teaching force. That underscores how educational justice must be about civil rights. W. E. B. Du Bois said that it was a Negro idea in the South that the government should provide education for black children. We birthed that idea out of the pain and struggle for our humanity. As black access to quality education improved in the 1970s and 1980s—which was also the height of unionization—the achievement gap between black and white students closed dramatically. Then suddenly, in response to the economic and academic gains that black people were achieving, the system reset itself, beginning with mayoral control and continuing through to budget cuts, privatization, school closures, and the growth of charter schools. The result has been devastating to black communities.

The power holders in this country have proven clever at finding ways to change the rules of the game to make it more difficult for black people to gain access to what should be guaranteed as a common good rather than a privilege. About 85 percent of the student population in Chicago is black or brown.[1] If you are not talking about racial justice, then you're not serious about transforming the education system to meet the needs of all students.

Our union has fought against the system for firing black teachers, for closing schools, for disinvesting in schools where the staff is overwhelmingly black, schools that were anchors in communities. We talk about the disproportionate impact that school closing has on black neighborhoods. It's not a coincidence that the same neighborhoods where schools are being attacked are also the most violent neighborhoods. These neighborhoods have suffered from a lack of affordable housing, lead paint contamination, and many other problems. They need more investment in education, not less.

If you're attacking public schools, you're attacking black people, especially women. Black women make up the large majority of recipients of teacher pensions. By going after our retirement security, the system is threatening resources that provide what little stability is left in many black neighborhoods. As a black man, I know that the economic security I have within the teaching profession didn't come just because someone thought it was a good idea to pay people more money. Black workers, who were not even accepted in the teachers' union in the early years, fought that struggle.

ORGANIZING AND FIGHTING

The history of black teachers is quite profound in this city. Black teachers struck as part of the CTU. But they also led wildcat strikes on their own, where they had to fight both the system and the union. We embrace that history of militant unionism.

The political and educational systems will not automatically provide the working and learning environment that we desire. There is only one way to achieve it: through organizing and fighting. That is not the most comfortable space for educators. It's hard enough to get through the daily routine of educating students. But the days of being able to simply close our doors and follow our lesson plans are over.

We can best support our students and our communities by organizing and fighting on their behalf. We showed teachers across the country that you can secure a good contract while also securing a good learning environment for students. It is worth that fight.

10

-o-o-o-o-o-o-

#ENDWARONYOUTH

Building a Youth Movement for
Black Lives and Educational Justice

– Jonathan Stith –

Alliance for Educational Justice, Washington, DC

Jonathan Stith talks about the efforts of the Alliance for Educational Justice, a coalition of youth organizing groups, to combat the school-to-prison pipeline. Formed in 2008, the alliance lobbied the Obama administration to take a stand against zero-tolerance school discipline practices and promote restorative justice alternatives. The murder of Trayvon Martin pushed the alliance toward a movement-building approach and a focus on police violence. As videos of widespread assaults by school police went viral, however, the alliance came to see the systemic nature of state violence, which amounted to a war on youth. The alliance demands the removal of police from schools and links the movement for black lives with the fight for educational justice and the liberation of youth of color.

I GOT INVOLVED IN youth organizing through working with young people in community service. I was trying to get students to clean up an area near their school that was dirty. They never wanted to do it, and I finally got fed up and asked what was wrong. They said, "What's the point? Someone will just dump here again next week." We called the community alliance for youth action and they organized the young people to take direct action: stake out the area, photograph the folks dumping, and confront the city council member from the district. They ended up getting the company cited and stopped the dumping.

In this moment I saw just how engaged and transformed the young folk were. This was way more exciting, way more engaging than service. It changed the whole paradigm: service was something you did when you got in trouble; organizing was something you did to improve your school and community and change the world.

Fast forward five or six years, and I was the executive director of a youth organizing group called the Youth Education Alliance. In 2008, the Gates Foundation invited youth organizing groups such as ours, which were doing education organizing across the country, to a meeting in New Orleans. The Gates folks had their agenda, but we took the opportunity to connect with each other. We were all talking about the same things, and we were some of the first groups to tackle the school-to-prison pipeline, with a focus on ending zero-tolerance school discipline practices.

The election happened, Obama won, and we saw an opportunity to shape federal policy. The Elementary and Secondary Education Act was up for reauthorization, and we had a Democratic Congress. We thought the political conditions were ripe for us to push federal policy with the idea that federal success would create more local opportunities for people in our communities. So, nineteen youth organizing groups came together to form the Alliance for Educational Justice (AEJ).

Reauthorization eventually went nowhere, but we found an opening to influence the Department of Education, which had expressed a desire to address the harmful effects of zero-tolerance school discipline policies. We worked with parent and community organizing groups in the Dignity in Schools Campaign, as well as with civil rights advocacy groups such as the Advancement Project and NAACP Legal Defense Fund. We got the department to require school districts to report on suspensions and expulsions, and to break out the data by race. The new data showed the incredible extent of the problem—3.5 million students were suspended from school each year, and they lost eighteen million days of instruction—and the racial disparities: black students were three times more likely to be suspended than white students.[1]

AEJ brought students to Washington to tell their personal stories of harsh and racist disciplinary practices, becoming the face behind the figures. We developed a comprehensive communication strategy to shift the narrative away from zero tolerance, operating as "critical allies" to officials on the inside of the Obama administration. Senator Dick Durbin called the first congressional hearing on the school-to-prison pipeline a historic moment when young people showed up en masse and testified before the US Senate about their experiences.

Eventually, all this work led the Department of Education and Department of Justice to issue joint guidance that warned school districts against excessive and racially inequitable school discipline practices and encouraged districts to adopt more positive behavioral and restorative justice alternatives.

This marked a dramatic shift in the public discourse away from harsh discipline; young people, parents, and their allies had changed the narrative and were driving a transformation in school discipline policy at local and state levels across the country. The acknowledgment of a school-to-prison pipeline was a huge victory because for many years educators denied that there was any such thing. We were told that we were crazy. So, when President Obama said the school-to-prison pipeline exists and must be addressed, that was huge.

When the Republicans took control of Congress after the 2010 midterm elections, the chance to push federal legislation was over. Our lobbying in Washington had also shown that we were not big enough: we didn't have local groups in all the districts whose representatives we needed to influence. We went through some internal restructuring and came out saying that we were going to become a movement-building alliance.

We weren't just education organizers; we were youth organizers. As Audre Lorde said, "There is no such thing as a single-issue struggle because we do not live single-issue lives."[2] For us that meant helping to start other national networks working on a range of issues. We played a big role in founding the Journey for Justice Alliance, which focused on stopping the massive school closings happening in black and brown communities in 2012. We joined the coordinating committee of the Alliance to Reclaim Our Schools, which includes teachers' unions, fights privatization of public education, and advocates for community schools.

TRAYVON MARTIN AND THE MOVEMENT FOR BLACK LIVES

The murder of Trayvon Martin was a movement-building moment and a turning point for AEJ. We were all together in Chicago at a Free Minds, Free Peoples conference when the verdict came out that the security guard who shot Trayvon, George Zimmerman, was acquitted. Fifty young people were literally stuffed into my hotel suite. They were really scared, they were terrified, they were heartbroken. It was just a lot of emotion in the room.

Meanwhile, Power U, our member group in Miami, and the Dream Defenders staged a dramatic sit-in protest at the state capitol, in Tallahassee. AEJ helped young people from New York, Baltimore, Philadelphia, and as far as away as California get on buses and planes to join them. AEJ ended up sending almost 150 high school students to stand with the Dream Defenders and Power U. That was a powerful movement-building moment for us when we said, "Y'all are not alone in this struggle." Young people understood that Trayvon could have been all of them or any one of them.

Soon after, we were in Miami for AEJ's national convening where a youth leader from Power U said, "I feel some kinda way that if Trayvon hadn't been suspended, he wouldn't never got killed that night." That landed on us like a ton of bricks. The young woman said that a security officer had found Trayvon with a bag that she said smelled like marijuana and he had a screwdriver on him. He was criminalized for this and suspended. This was his third time, and his mom felt like he needed a new start at a new place. That prompted her fateful decision to send Trayvon to live with his father, where he was subsequently shot and killed. Here it was: the impact of the school-to-prison pipeline and the connection to state violence.

The next year, George Carter was killed. George was a fifteen-year-old black student active as a youth leader in Rethink New Orleans, an AEJ member. George was killed on his way to school at seven in the morning in an overgrown field that hadn't been cut. After Hurricane Katrina, the school administration had closed the school in his neighborhood, so George and a whole bunch of other young folks had to get up at the crack of dawn and catch a bus to the other side of New Orleans to go to school, and he was killed in an act of intercommunal violence. The New Orleans police put out a story in the newspaper that he was killed because he was part of a gang that was robbing a store, that he might have been killed because he was involved in a corner-store robbery.

We said, "God, even in our death, we are criminalized." It confirmed for us that it doesn't matter if you're a good black kid or a troubled black kid. This is a state of war that's happening. This doesn't happen to white kids. The murder of a white boy would have been seen as a tragedy. He would have been lifted up in his best light and remembered for all that he was—not criminalized as George was.

I have a deep personal connection with George because he was one of the first young people I met in New Orleans when we were trying to recruit Rethink to join AEJ. George was a special young person, and yet he was killed and criminalized.

FERGUSON AND CALLING FOR AN END TO THE 1033 PROGRAM

Then, eighteen-year-old Michael Brown was killed in Ferguson, Missouri. Once again, young people saw one of their peers get shot down by police. Mike Brown's mom lamented about how difficult it had been to get him to graduate from high school, a school where over 50 percent of students get pushed out.

I went to Ferguson with youth leaders from AEJ groups and another organizer from Philadelphia, Hiram Rivera, to work with the Organization for Black Struggle to help support youth organizing. We saw the pain. We saw the military-grade weapons. We saw the tanks. And we found out that these tanks and guns came from the federal government through its 1033 program, which supplies excess military equipment to police departments. Youth leaders and organizers from the Labor Community Strategy Center in Los Angeles were with us. They returned home and found out that their school police had been receiving equipment from the 1033 program, including semiautomatic weapons and a tank! We learned that school police in Miami and New York were getting weapons from 1033 as well.

We also saw that the same police officers who were killing black men on the street were assaulting peaceful protestors. Ferguson reminded us of Soweto in 1966, where South African police attacked and massacred children marching to protest apartheid.

In response, we demanded that the Obama administration end the 1033 program. In May of 2015, the administration did set some restrictions on the program, although it did not eliminate it. But youth leaders in LA successfully pressured the school district to return the tank and M-16 rifles.

SPRING VALLEY—CALLING FOR POLICE OUT OF SCHOOLS

Then the assault at Spring Valley, South Carolina, happened in which a school police officer grabbed a black girl named Shakara by the neck and body-slammed and dragged her while she was sitting at her desk. It was recorded by students in the class. Another black student, Niya Kenny, tried to intervene and told the officer to stop; she was arrested and charged with "disrupting school." The recording went viral and became a national flash point.

Young people in five cities began to organize and wrote love letters and letters of support to Shakara and Niya by the hundreds. Niya came to a national meeting sponsored by the Funders Collaborative for Youth Organizing in Durham, North Carolina. The students got up on stage and read the letters to Niya. It was a really emotional and powerful moment. They declared themselves part of the Drop the Charges Campaign in support of Niya and Shakara, and committed to figuring out how to build a national campaign to get police out of schools.

The campaign to support Niya and Shakara became part of the black girls matter moment—the recognition that it's not just black and brown boys who are targeted by police and end up in the school-to-prison pipeline. Meanwhile, we launched our #EndWarOnYouth campaign on December 18, 2015, and young people in six cities held "die-ins."

RAPID RESPONSE AND SYSTEMIC CHANGE

More videos of police attacks kept surfacing, and we developed a code, the "assault at," where we insert the school name, like "assault at Spring Valley." By an *assault at* we mean an act of state-sanctioned violence by a police officer at a school.

We started to build a rapid-response campaign and would go to places where *assault at*'s occurred to support the victims, help organize a response, and publicize the effort across the country to build national support. But we realized that we needed to press for changes in policy and systems beyond responding to the individual *assault at*.

In 2016, at Ben Franklin High School in Philadelphia, a student named Brian, who was involved with the Philadelphia Student Union, was punched, thrown to the floor, and put in a choke hold by a school police officer for trying to go to the bathroom without a hall pass. A student who recorded the event was told to delete the footage.

We realized that *assault at*'s were actually just the tip of the iceberg of a huge system of racist policing in our schools. We were finding out how unregulated school police departments were. There's no visible complaint system. There's very little data. It's hidden. Some school districts do not keep a record of arrests.

The young people in the Philadelphia Student Union, a founding AEJ member, mounted a really impressive seven-week campaign to support Brian and press for broader change. They convinced the school superintendent to agree to reduce the number of uniformed officers in schools, guarantee at least one nurse and one counselor in every school, and create a system for filing complaints against police abuse in schools.

In January of 2016, Niya Kenny and several youth leaders from New Orleans testified in Jackson, Mississippi, in front of a UN Commission that was touring the US holding hearings on the status of people of African descent. They spoke about the school-to-prison pipeline and their experiences with police in schools. The UN commission ended up calling for the removal of police from schools in the US, as well as making a number of additional recommendations to combat the school-to-prison pipeline and other forms of racial discrimination.[3] It was a huge win for us in terms of pushing the dialogue and winning the war of ideas that police don't belong in schools. We got it in the UN record that, in fact, the police presence in schools violates human rights charters on children and education.

Whenever black and brown youth push for bold changes, they are told it cannot be done. We proved them wrong with ending zero tolerance in school discipline, and we will prove them wrong with getting police out of schools.

In November of 2017, in response to organizing by the Movement for Black Lives in Toronto, Canada, the school board canceled its contract with the Toronto School Police Department and removed all uniformed police officers from their schools. That was huge for us because it showed schools do not have to have police.

After the school shooting in Parkland, Florida, in 2018, it became all the more critical for us to resist a push for more police and repressive discipline in schools and to join with the movement for gun control and restorative approaches. Our young folks have heartfelt sympathy for the young people in Parkland, but they are also very angry at the contradictions that exist around gun violence. When nineteen black youth died in one weekend in Chicago, nobody cared. Nobody wants to talk about gun violence until white kids kill themselves.

STATE VIOLENCE AND BLACK LIVES

Organizers like me have now come to the point where we see the intimate connection between the movement for black lives, the school-to-prison pipeline, police in schools, and educational justice. We are fighting an entire system of criminalization, militarization, and state-sponsored violence that amounts to a war on youth.

So, we fight on many fronts and bring an intersectional approach that connects and confronts the issues and systems that oppress youth. Along with other AEJ leaders, I became part of the Black Organizing for Leadership and Dignity group, which is building a new infrastructure for black social justice organizing. Hiram Rivera and I cowrote the education policy platform for the Movement for Black Lives, calling for an end to the privatization of public education, a moratorium on out-of-school suspensions, the removal of police from schools, democratic community control of schools, and, more broadly, the liberation of black education and of black peoples.

#EndWarOnYouth is a multiracial campaign. The state violence that black youth experience, though it has its own special venom, is felt by brown students, is felt by immigrant students, and is felt by LGBTQ youth. AEJ is multiracial and includes diverse youth. But we are clear that black youth are central to ending the war on youth.

I feel honored and blessed to do the work I do with young folk. I see myself as carrying on the tradition of Ella Baker, and that feels really sacred. Young people speak truth to power. They are willing to take risks and to say things that may not be polite but that start to disrupt deep-seated racist practices. By their bold actions they move decision makers to take young people seriously and to take their vision for education seriously. I have been proud to stand beside these great young folk, to dream with them, and then to try to make that dream come true in the world.

PART THREE

EDUCATORS FOR JUSTICE

Movement Building in Schools, School Systems, and Universities

11

--o--o--o--o--o--o--

TEACHERS UNITE!

Organizing School Communities
for Transformative Justice

– Sally Lee and Elana "E. M." Eisen-Markowitz –

Teachers Unite, New York City

Sally Lee and Elana "E. M." Eisen-Markowitz talk about the role of teachers as key participants in the fight for educational justice. Frustrated with the racist history of the local teachers' union in New York City, Sally founded Teachers Unite to organize and support teachers as agents of democratic change in their union and allies for racial justice in schools and communities. E. M. shows how teachers can partner with students and their families to create restorative justice programs that transform relationships, culture, and practices in school communities. While winning changes in policy is necessary, Sally and E. M. highlight the essential role of school-site organizing that engages educators to create deep and sustainable transformative justice for young people.

> We must do battle where we are standing.[1]
>
> —AUDRE LORDE

SALLY'S STORY

Education is a big deal in my family. I'm a black multiracial woman from a middle-class, downtown Manhattan background. My father and his four siblings were first-generation college graduates who grew up poor and black in New England. My grandfather never attended college; he had been a talent scout, numbers runner, waiter, and bank security guard, among other professions. At night, after working as a guard, he studied my dad's college economics textbooks and surpassed the white bankers in a professional advancement course. He went on to become the first black bank manager in western Massachusetts. In my family it was a given that each of us was smart and capable, and the fact that white people dominated institutions was simply proof of racism and oppression. We proved this through our academic achievement and by being a barrier-breaking family of "firsts."

The emphasis on school in my upbringing cannot be overstated. We believed in the importance of quality, integrated schools in creating a just society, and I wanted to understand and improve how that happened. As a young adult, I knew that I wanted to work in education and make big systemic changes—and I knew I had to start that journey in the classroom.

I began teaching fifth and sixth grades in the Lower East Side in Manhattan, which is adjacent to my own childhood neighborhood and was always my favorite place in the world. (It has now been my home for eleven years.) My students looked like the neighborhood: mostly Puerto Rican and Dominican, but also black, white, Mexican, and Chinese. Increasing gentrification in the neighborhood, however, meant that younger grades were looking whiter and whiter. About half of my students' parents needed Spanish-English translation to communicate with me, but the PTA leaders were virtually all white, native English speakers. The new parent leadership seemed to mark a shift away from the neighborhood's long history of polyglot immigration, creativity, and guerilla-style land reclamation. Instead, diversity was talked about as one describes a box of crayons.

While I loved working with children, I was demoralized that my racially diverse colleagues, who were light-years ahead of me as pedagogues (I was a fumbling, bumbling new teacher), seemed unconcerned about the increasing marginalization of our students of color. The families of my students most in need of a village of advocates were not included in school leadership. I quickly became consumed both with my inability to be that village on my own and with the seeming absence of social justice teacher organizing in my city.

Founding Teachers Unite

Through my own research, I learned that in the 1930s the Teachers Union (TU) of New York City was known for its militant activism and worked with parents and community groups in Harlem to protest the brutal treatment of black students. When I quit teaching to start a teachers' organization, I named it Teachers Unite (TU), partly in homage to the earlier TU.

We started TU in 2006 with a mission to organize democratic school chapters under the principles of equity, voice, diversity, and action, with an eye toward changing society and building a center for radical teacher organizing. The teachers' union local, the United Federation of Teachers (UFT), had an infamous history of conflict with communities of color dating back to its opposition to black community demands for local control of schools in the 1960s. We founded TU to try to build analysis and power among an intergenerational group of educators with a vision of democratically transforming the UFT into an ally in fights for racial and economic justice in schools and communities.

Teachers Talk

In pursuit of this mission, TU has launched a variety of projects and campaigns since its founding. Through building relationships with organizations fighting the school-to-prison pipeline, we copublished *Teachers Talk: School Culture, Safety, and Human Rights* with the National Economic and Social Rights Initiative (NESRI) in 2008. We surveyed more than 300 middle and high school teachers in more than 130 public schools across New York City and found that, contrary to what many people thought, many teachers had critical views of harsh discipline policies. Almost two-thirds of teachers felt that armed police officers in the school never or rarely made students feel safe. Half said that students should have "a lot" or "the most" influence over discipline and safety policies. Many teachers wanted support for students rather than punishment, like this Manhattan science teacher: "There should be a room with counselors or social workers where I could say to a kid, 'Go now and talk to Mrs. So and So.' . . . With certain kids, they need a chance to walk it off. . . . There are all these obstacles to getting them the help they need. And then I hear that, next period, the kid got suspended for yelling at a teacher, and I think, 'Well, no wonder.'"[2]

The teachers we surveyed were not using terms like "restorative justice" as many do today, but they were thoughtful and concerned about the harmful effects of zero tolerance. As recently as November 2016, the American Federation of Teachers requested to review information from *Teachers Talk*—arguably because no one, including the union, has asked rank-and-file educators what they think about school safety. From *Teachers Talk*, TU recognized a need and a potential to build with students and families with the goal of interrupting the criminalization of people of color in NYC. Our partnership with NESRI introduced us to the Dignity in Schools Campaign (DSC), a national coalition of grassroots and advocacy groups working to end the school-to-prison pipeline. TU joined DSC and got involved in its local New York chapter; we remain the only educator group member to this day.

Toolkits for Educators

After *Teachers Talk*, TU focused on building our network of educators growing restorative justice (RJ) at their schools. Meanwhile, our DSC partners and educators across the city were asking us if we could put them in touch with these schools or help duplicate their work. In 2013 TU campaign coordinator Anna Bean suggested a film project that would document strategies used by schools to try to meet students' needs rather than just punishing them. We convened our member-leaders to plan *Growing Fairness*, a documentary and online toolkit focused on building the capacity of schools to resist the racist criminalization of students. Thousands of people viewed the film in its first year, and we continue to sell dozens of copies each year across the country. The project helped increase press coverage of RJ and launched TU as a go-to teachers' organization on the topic. Meanwhile, we committed ourselves to support member-leaders to collaboratively build RJ strategies at their schools.

It took years for TU to arrive collectively at a theory of social change that centers school-site organizing and a functional plan for supporting it. It is much easier to be a supportive community of like-minded folks outside of schools than it is to organize those folks to do the hard work of building relationships with coworkers who may be exhausted, overwhelmed, unappreciated, ignorant, or oppositional. TU members' roles as public school workers inform our relational approach to organizing: in a functioning democracy, we must slowly build consensus among diverse individuals around core values in order to transform culture. I have never heard a teacher say that students started thriving in a punitive school because of a few teacher allies, but I have heard multiple stories, like E. M.'s below, that describe years of collaborative hard work forging a new road map for a school community that empowers student leaders.

Redefining Worker Organizing and Teacher Unionism

The disgraceful legacy of undemocratic, racist teachers' unions and the present-day reality of school-based oppression have meant that our organizational allies in DSC almost never think to reach out to rank-and-file teachers as potential allies. Instead, the strategy has been to confront districts around the country and fight for discipline policy changes and mandates without including teachers at all. While these policy changes are necessary, they will not meaningfully change the experiences of young people in schools if there is no buy-in or support from their teachers. Districts under fire are only too happy to offer multimillion-dollar contracts to nonprofit vendors who nominate themselves to train staff, usually without adequate plans or any educator input. The New York City mayor's office and his appointed chancellor are claiming lowered suspension rates or successful implementation of RJ district-wide across the city, but our members often tell a different story. They speak about nonprofit consultants who come and go suddenly and/or waste educators' time. They are hurt and angry that their black and brown students are once again being treated like guinea pigs in a rushed initiative created for political purposes. Our members end up frustrated by being stuck in the middle of a co-opted agenda that cares nothing about centering the voices or experiences of young people and their families, and that does nothing to build power or reflection among school staff.

The oppressive history of public schools requires a seismic shift in how we go about transforming school culture and education policy. By focusing on school-site organizing, TU is trying to redefine worker organizing and teacher unionism as well as the power relationships within each school's community.

E.M.'S STORY

For better or worse, schools are often the places where people learn how to *be* in the world—they are reflections of the problems and the potential of our society. As a queer, white, Jewish kid, I was politicized by my experiences growing up middle class and navigating diverse, divided public schools in and around Washington, DC, in the 1980s and 1990s. I was prohibited from performing with a grade-school chorus because I did not wear a dress, and the following year I enlisted seven other girls to boycott dresses for the performance too. I wondered why so few of my classmates of color were in my middle or high school "honors" classes and watched friends of color get stopped constantly by school security when I could walk in and out of the building freely—and then cowrote a series of articles for the school newspaper about racial profiling and tracking in our high school. All my life, I have seen and felt how schools can be sites of trauma and oppression as well as sites of meaningful growth and change. I am a teacher because I believe in the power we have to change ourselves and the people closest to us.

Building the Foundations for Restorative Justice

On a rainy Wednesday afternoon in April, I sat in room 303 at the very end of the school day, recording and clarifying the notes from the day's Restorative Justice Action Team (RJAT) meeting. Seven staff and five students had just shown up to a bimonthly after-school meeting about how to implement restorative justice practices in our alternative public school that serves sixteen- to twenty-one-year-olds in New York City. We were on the verge of proposing our comprehensive, multi-stakeholder plan to integrate restorative justice meaningfully at our school. Though I was cautiously hopeful, I had been feeling drained by the daily work of teaching that feels like harm reduction most days—important for individuals' survival but not always toward transformative visioning or deep relationships; work that may be centered on feeding and caring for young people but is not really about shifting power.

Before that rainy Wednesday, RJAT spent a year and a half organizing our school community in order to lay a foundation for restorative justice (RJ). When they transfer to our school, students have faced problems that are seen across New York City's high schools: harsh and racially discriminatory disciplinary policies that lead to excessive suspensions and expulsions, the less tangible effects of police presence and metal detectors, as well as many more informal practices that lead to school pushout. We were ready to explore RJ as a real alternative that could help us get at the root causes of the school-to-prison pipeline, help students and staff form healthy relationships, and learn to resolve conflicts in ways that transform power dynamics.

TU uses both "restorative justice" and "transformative justice" as terms for our work, although "transformative justice" perhaps more accurately acknowledges the role and history of institutional oppression and emphasizes that we must move forward rather than attempt simply to "restore" what was there before. Both restorative and transformative justice are concerned with the *process* of growing justice as well as its results. As the school-to-prison pipeline becomes a catchphrase, many districts are mandating RJ as a "classroom management" strategy when it really needs to be a philosophical paradigm shift. If we want RJ to shift school culture and policies, we need to create a sustained organizing process at the school site that includes staff, families, and students.

In room 303 we laid this foundation by building the RJAT from a study group of about eight staff members, four students, and two parents who met to explore theories and practices of restorative and transformative justice in schools. Members of the group met over the summer to design professional development for staff and brainstorm ways to grow familiarity with restorative practices at our school. We designed courses that would establish critical foundational knowledge, and two students committed to co-facilitating a course with me about the school-to-prison pipeline. We attended trainings offered by the NYC Department of Education and shared what we learned with our colleagues. We facilitated staff meetings based on role plays, surveys, and community-building circles to communicate to staff the deep philosophical shift RJ would require. I met with staff who wanted to try restorative interventions with young people who were having conflict and needed support. We pushed back against our well-meaning administration and colleagues who wanted to move too quickly toward "restorative" protocols for students without the structure or culture of self-reflection from school staff.

Allying with Students, Families, and Communities

And now we're here—a committed, intergenerational group of teachers, counselors, school staff, and young people—visioning for the collaborative, justice-oriented future of our school. We could not have gotten here without my organizing with TU and our partners in DSC over the last eight years. My training, learning, and deeply relational organizing with TU has shaped what I believe is possible in schools. Moreover, it has introduced us to the language and strategies of the movement to dismantle the school-to-prison pipeline, to models of transformational healing and safety without police, and to the expertise of many people who have been doing this work for much longer than we have. Because of our connections to TU and DSC, we know when the Department of Education revises the discipline code and how to leverage new changes with our principal to invest in more counselors for our students. We know how to help our school leadership team rewrite our Comprehensive Education Plan to focus on evaluating racial disparities and increasing parent involvement.

Now it's noon on a Thursday in mid-June, and room 303 is packed. About thirty-five out of fifty educators are waiting to cast a vote that would create a new, full-time "RJ coordinator" staff position as a key part of our plan for a set of whole-school shifts: in- and out-of-school credit-bearing internships for student RJ leaders, RJ-focused parent orientations, and schedule changes that would free students and teachers up for community building. Union rules require that at least 51 percent of the staff must vote to create a full-time out-of-classroom position like an RJ coordinator. As a result, very few schools have RJ coordinators; skillful, time-intensive, school-site organizing is necessary in order to make it happen. In room 303 on this day, the vote was unanimous: all staff members who showed up agreed to commit resources for an RJ coordinator at our school.

Schools as Sites for Liberation

School-site organizing, like true transformation and healing, is slow and neither linear nor hierarchical. It looks different in different places. It's based on a decentralized cycle of leadership development that requires many different invested leaders who learn from and challenge one another. It wasn't until May of this school year—when I realized that eight members of my school community, ages sixteen to sixty-five, had written pieces of our school-wide proposal—that I believed my school would be ready to meaningfully shift toward transformative justice. So I agreed to become the RJ coordinator. I wouldn't do it without a core of people who understand how hard the work will be to chip away at our own biases and the school system's entrenched racism.

This is the second NYC public school I've worked at in eleven years where I have organized with staff, teachers, parents, and students not just to demand a change in our policies but also to build the knowledge, skills, and engagement to make those changes real. I don't know if it's possible to transform US public schools as an institution, but I do think it is possible to organize and shift power at the school site to change things materially for young people and their families and for staff. Why wouldn't we want to try that? Young people are required by law to be at school. Does this mean that school will *never* be a site of liberation or that we *must* make it a site for liberation? If our fights begin where we are standing, we can't afford *not* to call one another to transform ourselves and our schools.

SALLY AND E. M.'S REFLECTION: TRANSFORMATIVE JUSTICE

> All fights begin where you are. . . . We have to be careful not
> to underestimate the power we have in our neighborhoods,
> in our places of worship, in our schools.
>
> —EVE L. EWING[3]

When we dream of how to make systemic change, we envision working with young people, families, neighborhoods, and communities at our schools. The school itself, however, is its own community, village, and workplace. We need to recognize the harm committed by our colleagues and act to transform relationships while we create processes and structures for those harmed to imagine new solutions. Deep and sustainable transformative justice needs to be built school by school. An educational justice movement guided by principles of democracy and equity needs to support members of school communities to lead the way.

12

◦—◦—◦—◦—◦—◦—◦

CAN SCHOOLS NURTURE THE SOULS OF BLACK AND BROWN CHILDREN?

Combating the School-to-Prison Pipeline in Early Childhood Education

– Roberta Udoh –

Young Achievers Science and Math Pilot School,
Boston, Massachusetts

Roberta Udoh talks about her role as a black pre-K teacher committed to working with families, other teachers, students, and community activists to create schools in which black and brown children can flourish. As a union and community activist, she organizes to advocate for the school district to provide the resources and adopt the policies needed for schools to serve the holistic needs of urban children. In her classroom, she broadens the Eurocentric focus of the curriculum in order to nourish the souls of black and brown children, feed their psyches, and support their families. Roberta reflects on the role that teachers must play both in and out of the classroom as profound agents of social justice in the lives of children.

I GREW UP IN what can only be described as abject poverty in North London. The majority of students in my school were very poor, like my family, or living in homeless shelters. But the 1960s was an interesting time in public education. The school district where we lived was very progressive and innovative.

The schools offered a child-centered, progressive education that was part of a political agenda by the Labour Party aimed at lifting poor people out of poverty. The Labour Party was also building public housing and expanding national health care. There were social workers and nurses at my school. The meals were delicious and nutritional, which I remember because my brothers and I were dependent on those school meals.

I remember one of my elementary teachers, Ms. Woods at the Gillespie Primary School. She used a progressive, multicultural curriculum that was ahead of its time. I learned to sing social protest songs from the antipoverty marches of the 1930s in England. I also learned gospel spirituals. We learned about the US civil rights movement, the Atlantic slave trade, colonialism, and child labor during Victorian times, as well as the progressive movement that fought to give children the opportunity to be children.

The academic standard at Gillespie was very high. We read a lot. We had a lot of discussion about issues affecting children, and there was a lot of dialogue between students and teachers. We did a reenactment of the Aztec encounter with Europeans from the Aztec point of view and a reenactment of the colonization of Africa from the African point of view. We had lots of music and art. The school exposed us to cultures outside our experience to help us develop intellectually and emotionally.

My experience at Gillespie provides the model for me as a teacher today. I want my school to have the same kind of commitment to lift up poor children and children of color, to help them grow intellectually and socially-emotionally, and to teach them about systems of oppression and how people have fought against them.

DON'T BE "ONE OF THEM"

My decision to become a teacher was both personal and political. When my two daughters attended public schools in Cambridge, Massachusetts, I volunteered in the classroom and became active in the Parent Teacher Organization. The more involved I got, the more I became aware of the apartheid nature of the schools in Cambridge—how white and black children were treated quite differently. By the time our oldest daughter was in middle school, the administrators came down hard with discipline on black students and alienated them from school. I also started to think that maybe I could be a classroom teacher and do things differently.

At the time, I was working for Girls' LEAP (Lifetime Empowerment and Awareness Program), an all-women's organization that taught a violence-prevention curriculum to school-age girls. Girls' LEAP helped girls deal with the misogyny and sexism in society, especially the violence that girls experience in schools. I became deeply concerned about the low standard of education girls received in urban public schools and their feeling that schools didn't care about them.

When I asked a group of girls from Roxbury to write in their journals about their experiences, one fifth-grader asked me, "How do I spell 'cat'?" I took a quick survey and discovered that many of the girls were not spelling or reading at grade level. One group of high school girls from East Boston told me, "Our schools suck. Our teachers are useless, and they don't care about us."

That's when I decided to become a teacher. However, most of the girls were opposed to the idea. They were concerned that I would become like "one of them," meaning teachers who didn't care about them, who looked down on them because they were poor or of color or didn't come from what was perceived as functional families, and who didn't take their voices seriously. To hear this was profoundly sad to me, because my own schooling experience had been quite the opposite.

I have always kept in the forefront of my teaching not to become "one of them."

BRINGING ACTIVISM INTO TEACHING

I blend my life and work experiences with my activism and bring them into my teaching practices. I always ask myself, How would students and families receive this? I work with a prescribed curriculum that doesn't always align with my teaching philosophy, but I try to weave in other agendas. For example, I try to focus on issues of identity, such as how black and brown children or poor children see themselves, even as young as three.

I did my student teaching in a fourth-grade classroom in a Boston public school, where I designed a unit on child labor that the students loved. We studied photos by Louis Hine, who was a photographer for the National Child Labor Committee in the early 1900s. I also taught a unit on Cape Verdean sailors who were the backbone of the whaling industry in New England. We went on a trip to the New Bedford Whaling Museum, and the kids loved it—especially the Cape Verdean students. This kind of enrichment is essential to connecting learning to the souls of black and brown children.

While teaching fourth grade, I decided that there was absolutely no way I could administer the Massachusetts Comprehensive Assessment System, the annual statewide assessment test. I saw how it impacted students' emotional and psychological well-being. Children started to doubt their intellectual capacity, further alienating them from school and learning.

I looked for a grade where I wouldn't have to assess students in that way. I tried kindergarten but discovered that kindergarten is now the new first grade, where students can no longer engage in purposeful creative play that feeds their imagination and psyche. So I switched to teaching pre-K, and my classroom is known as the Guppy classroom. As children come into the institution of school, I've been able to lessen the impact of a dysfunctional school district like Boston and try to make their learning joyful. I use a lot of hands-on activities. I do a lot of nature activities with the Guppies, and I've been fortunate to be able to partner with the Audubon Society's Boston Nature Center, where we go on field trips. We also have a classroom garden, and we talk about the importance of growing things and taking care of the natural world.

All children need to experience intellectual ideas outside of their normal worldview. I try to replicate the kinds of school experiences that I had as a child, nurturing student curiosity and making learning meaningful and joyful. This is especially important for children with distressing lives, including those who are homeless or dealing with violence.

I try to fill their souls and make the world look beautiful to them. Ultimately, all children are extremely curious, so eventually their curiosity takes over and they start participating. Even the most depressed children will start engaging with their peers if learning is accessible to them and joyful.

"TO KNOW THE CHILD, YOU MUST KNOW THE FAMILY"

Without the support of families, I couldn't achieve much in the classroom. In my curriculum-night presentation, I tell families, "I have your child for a year. You have your child for the rest of their lives. What can I truly accomplish in a year without your support?"

I have to show families in my everyday teaching practices that I'm deeply committed to the well-being of their child. From the start, I make it clear to families that I am always open to them. This is not *my* classroom. It's *their* classroom.

To know the child, you must know the family. I get to know the family in a way that is nonthreatening. I make home visits. Before I visit, I tell families, "Please don't clean your house for me or lay out any food. I'm not social services coming in. We're just going to have a chat about what you expect of me as a teacher in the upcoming year."

I ask questions of families. I don't lecture. I explain the curriculum and show parents where they can look it up online. I give away as much information as possible. I don't hoard information, which can sometimes happen with teachers trying to protect their power.

Parents need to become advocates for their children. Urban school districts do not have the resources to provide all the supports that students need nor the extracurricular activities that middle-class families have. Parents must advocate for services or activities in the school. I tell them, "Join the parent council, and demand your rights."

I encourage families to see themselves as their child's teacher. So I share with families what I have learned as a paid educator. That's the kind of advocacy that I try to do with families, and then I support the family's advocacy when they speak up for their child.

THE SCHOOL-TO-PRISON PIPELINE STARTS IN PRE-K

I believe that the school-to-prison pipeline starts in pre-K. The district does not provide the resources and support staff, such as counselors and social workers, that teachers need to address all the social-emotional issues children bring into class that can lead to "misbehavior." Racial and gender bias and cultural incompetence are big parts of the problem. When poor black or brown children act up, they are seen as "troublemakers" and sent out into the hall or even suspended; when suburban white children do the same thing, they are called "precocious." Black and brown boys especially are disciplined rather than supported to channel their energy into positive learning.

Schools of higher education are an important part of the problem, because they just churn out early childhood educators like in sausage factories, credentialing teachers who don't understand that the needs of poor children of color are completely different from the needs of white middle-class kindergartners. The teaching model is based on middle-class students and the assumption that when children come to pre-K, they are "ready to learn."

That means they can sit and listen to a story, they can be safe with their bodies, and they can speak simple sentences.

The reality is that the "ready to learn" gap is profound. For example, I've had pre-K kids who cannot speak a full sentence at age three. They just say one word: "Ball." "Table." "Chair."

Teachers who lack cultural competence label these children as "slow" and do not know how to support the students and their families. I have seen many cases where teachers push these children out of the classroom and they wander around the halls. They are not officially suspended, but they are excluded. This is the beginning of the school-to-prison pipeline for these children.

Teachers do not pay enough attention to the important role of families. You can work with families to achieve tremendous growth in a child in a short period of time. In my classroom, I've seen that you can change even the most challenging child in a few months if you have families supporting and teaching you about their child.

There is also the issue of cultural competency with regard to children's families. Teachers cannot assume that families can sit down and read to their children for twenty minutes every day. Single moms don't even have twenty minutes to themselves when they come home. So I encourage them to read when they can and suggest books for them to use, but I don't assume anything or judge parents.

Other contributors to the school-to-prison pipeline are the lack of resources for students in schools and poverty in the community. There is a history of institutionalized racism and segregation in the Boston Public Schools. In 2016 Boston cut millions of dollars to schools, and we have a mayor, Marty Walsh, who's increasingly gentrifying communities, so housing is really tough for a lot of working-poor families. Some families have to move in with grandparents or aunts and uncles, which can contribute to a more distressed family home life.

TEACHERS AS EDUCATION ACTIVISTS

These are exciting times for teachers' unions. We now have models of unions working with communities and partnering with families and students to fight for resources and to promote restorative justice and positive behavior intervention and supports. The Chicago Teachers Union is leading this effort.

There is a growing critical mass of activists in the Boston Teachers Union (BTU) who are concerned about these issues too. In 2017 we elected a new president, Jessica Tang, and a slate of officers for the BTU that reflect the growing movement in unions to not just protect educators but to honor the voices of families and students too. In the past, educators have unfortunately seen families and students as uncaring and part of the problem; the new movement sees them as powerful partners in education and social change.

Being active in my union connects me. It takes me outside of the classroom, which can be isolating. As soon as the school day starts, I'm focused intently on my classroom. My union activism keeps me informed and connected to what is happening in other schools across the district and beyond.

I'm active on union committees, including the Early Childhood Education and Inclusion and Special Education committees. I bring not just my voice but also the voices of families and students to those spaces. We are working hard to address the racial and class inequities in the school district.

I am also active in the Boston Education Justice Alliance, which has been a real soul saver for me. BEJA gives me a space to connect with my deepest values. I get to connect with educators, other activists, and families and students from across the district. I get to hear what they're dealing with and what they are doing.

Through BEJA I became involved in the Save Our Public Schools campaign. It was a campaign against charter school expansion, and we won! We stopped a corporate-funded ballot initiative that would have led to defunding public schools in Boston and eventually closing many of them. I met an incredible number of families and young people who were investing so much time and energy on this campaign, going door-to-door in the heat of summer in the fight for public education.

I also worked with BEJA to start a petition campaign against budget cuts in Boston Public Schools. The proposed cuts were devastating. Thousands of people signed the petition I wrote and sent out through MoveOn. org. However, it was the young people who organized a day of action when we protested outside city hall and delivered the petition to Boston mayor Marty Walsh. It was a powerful event, because we were all in alignment.

Families, educators, community activists, and young people gathered at the state house and city hall to say, "We're against these cuts and we want quality schools."

That was a turning point for many of us, because we realized the potential for building alliances across the city.

SILENCING

I teach at Young Achievers Science and Math Pilot School, where I feel I have found a school with a commitment to social justice that honors all voices. But even here, there are challenges.

I can't always talk about race and class with my teaching colleagues. As a person of African descent, this challenge is very personal for me. I recently had an experience where I silenced myself because I thought, "It's going to take too much energy to explain to this white teacher why some of her teaching practices are culturally incompetent."

Many educators of color experience this kind of silencing, and it eats away at your soul. I have to feed my soul so that it doesn't get depleted. That's why I work on my activism inside and outside of the school. I have built alliances with supportive administrators and with other teachers in the school, so we have a stronger voice than that of the teachers who lack cultural competency. Our school is finding it harder and harder to hire teachers who are in alignment with its social justice values, because higher education doesn't make the issues of race, class, and equity a priority in training teachers.

In order to create a climate where children don't feel like they have to keep quiet about who they are, we must have a top-down policy to dismantle institutional racism. That has to be coupled with the bottom-up voices of families, students, and community activists who must participate in those policy discussions.

I am deeply concerned that more and more of our black and brown children are giving up on school because they feel silenced. Their social and emotional needs are not being met. Their psyche is not being nurtured. The typical approach to social-emotional learning is really about managing kids' challenges so that they can carry out meaningless lessons, instead of enriching their lives by teaching the whole child, giving them exciting experiences and meaningful field trips, like to the Boston Nature Center.

What students get in an affluent suburb like Brookline, Massachusetts, should be what students in Boston get, both inside and outside of school. This requires money and resources. And it requires a vision of the kind of citizen you are preparing your student to be: is it someone who's intellectually engaged with the world or just prison fodder? We can teach children to read, but what's the point if we're only preparing them to be passive consumers rather than fighters for social justice?

These are societal issues that will not be solved solely within schools. We have to take action to create a society that meets the needs of all children—in the community and in the school. We teachers have a critical role to play as educators and activists to support our children and families and to feed the souls of our students.

13

SYSTEM CHANGE

Following an Inside-Outside Strategy as a School Board Member

– Mónica García –

*Board of Education,
Los Angeles Unified School District*

When Mónica García was elected to the LA Unified School District Board of Education in 2006, she was only the third Latina to hold the position in 155 years. Mónica is part of a new generation of Latino/a activists who work across racial lines for bold, systemic change. Over the course of a decade, this alliance of parents, youth, community groups, unions, and elected officials transformed the school district in profound ways, increasing graduation rates, reducing zero-tolerance disciplinary practices, and increasing access to college. Mónica discusses the inside-outside strategy at the heart of the alliance's successes and reflects on the necessity to persevere for the long struggle needed to create meaningful opportunities for all students.

THE LOS ANGELES UNIFIED SCHOOL DISTRICT (LAUSD) is on the front line of the fight for justice and access to quality schools for people of color and low-income families. The *Mendez v. Westminster* (1947) case, which ended racial segregation in California, began the fight for all youth to have access to quality opportunities in our schools. As a person who benefited from the demand for access and quality, I joined with others who learned to read and write, think and believe, and banded together to change the second-largest school system in the country. We were bold, optimistic, and aggressive, and we knew we could change policy and practice in the LAUSD.

FROM THE COMMUNITY TO THE BOARD ROOM

Like so many children from East Los Angeles, I am the daughter of Mexican immigrants. My dad worked at the same manufacturing company for most of my young life. My mom stayed home and then eventually entered the labor market when the kids started school. I grew up surrounded by optimism and the belief that hard work and education bring opportunity.

When I was sixteen, I volunteered for the Southwest Voter Registration and Education Project, registering people to vote. As a seventh grader, I attended Youth Day Los Angeles, where I met Mayor Tom Bradley and was inspired by service in the public sector. I learned that certain people made big decisions that affected many others. I also learned that I had a responsibility to be civically active and that it took a lot of work to support a community.

I attended the University of California, Berkeley, from 1986 to 1991. Chicano/a students made up less than 1 percent of the student body at the time. There were massive campus-wide movements and work toward increasing diversity. I experienced a political awakening, as I came to understand how few Chicano/Latino students were making it to college. I loved Chicano studies, in which professors were mentors and models of courage. I learned that Chicanos are a community with a powerful history of resistance, persistence, struggle, and resilience.

I became a school counselor because I wanted to increase the number of young people who were prepared and purposefully investing in themselves through school and academic opportunities. I became an academic advisor with a human services organization called the Volunteers of America. Through their Talent Search program, I began my journey in LAUSD, serving two schools in South Los Angeles.

Latino/a students had horrible dropout rates at the time, with less than half of them graduating from high school. I felt LAUSD needed to learn about these students and their families and about how education is a powerful influence that can interrupt poverty. I had something to offer because of my personal experience and my strong belief that all children can learn. We just needed to change the opportunities in front of them and challenge the school system responsible for denying those opportunities.

In 2001 I became chief of staff to then LAUSD school board member José Huizar, representing District 2. This district extends from Koreatown through downtown and to unincorporated East LA, where the historic walkouts by Latino/a students protesting unequal conditions in schools took place in 1968.

Today each of the seven board districts has about 640,000 residents, so LA Unified is a massive system. LAUSD students today are 91 percent children of color and 74 percent Latino/a; 89 percent qualify for free or reduced price lunch.[1]

When we started working in District 2 in 2001, I would hear people in leadership say, "Kids don't want to," and "Kids can't," referencing students' abilities and potential. I rejected that narrative. I would hear leaders, board members, and superintendents say that a 45 percent graduation rate was not a crisis. I knew they were wrong.

My colleagues and I saw ourselves as change agents in the board member's office. We had an office of four Latinos with master's degrees, led by José, who had a master's degree from Princeton University and a law degree from UCLA. We could not support the status quo that denied opportunity to children. We wanted to open up LAUSD and get it to serve people better. Our strategy was not a one-school or a one-community solution. We knew that we were leaders for the entire district.

We developed an inside-outside strategy that consisted of standing up for beliefs that were challenging to the organization, making data public, and working side by side with community groups that were organizing on the ground to reform our schools.

BUILDING SCHOOLS

From 1980 to 2000 the number of students in LAUSD increased from five hundred thousand to approximately seven hundred thousand, yet for thirty-four years Los Angeles had not built any new schools.[2] Theodore Roosevelt High School, in my district, is a good example of the problem we faced. Roosevelt had over five thousand students. There was always a population of students that did extremely well—best in the nation. But a large majority didn't get the support they needed. We knew that Roosevelt had tried many ways to improve, but report after report said the size of the student body was just too large.

The leadership of LAUSD proposed the revolutionary idea of building 131 new schools and raising capital by issuing municipal bonds. We asked voters to tax themselves and make this money available to schools. In 2008 our efforts led to the passage of Measure Q, a $7 billion bond issue and the largest bond in US history at the time. We focused first on acknowledging that education and support services were not being provided equitably in our community. Second, we shared the stories of all the young people who wanted to be successful, who wanted access to a college preparatory curriculum and support with more counselors and tutoring. We had to debunk the idea that some children do not want to be learners. The bond program won support time after time, and LAUSD eventually created a $28 billion school construction program that changed our physical environment and engaged voters, civic leaders, community-based organization, unions, and parents and students in building space for learning.

EXPANDING COLLEGE ACCESS

In November 2005, José Huizar won a seat on the LA City Council. I ran for his school board seat and won in June 2006.

My interest in being a school board member came from the A-G Campaign of 2005. The A-G requirements comprise a list of courses that students must pass in high school for admission to California State University or the University of California. Many LA high schools did not offer all of these courses, such as the required advanced math course or a second year of world language. So even if you graduated from high school, you still were not eligible for entry to a four-year college.

The A-G Campaign was a movement led by young people demanding college access. Over the course of a year we built a citywide coalition of fifty community organizations, unions, and nonprofits to mobilize and lobby the district to offer the full range of A-G classes at all high schools. Over one thousand students and parents marched on the LAUSD offices and packed the boardroom, demanding rigor, access, and preparation for postsecondary education. There was authentic, organic leadership from the community. We held press conferences, wrote op-eds, collected signatures on petitions, and visited every school board official.

Teachers and elected officials came on board. We had representatives of the building trades step up and say our graduates struggled to fill out entry-level job applications. This was about system change and changing the belief that only some kids were meant to go to college.

To change the narrative about students of color, our community allies brought young people who were aspiring to go to college to testify and talk about how their schools needed to change. We had parents and students coming to say, "You, as leaders, have a responsibility." Following an inside-outside strategy once again, this broad coalition won, and the board adopted a resolution to bring A-G classes to all schools over time.

In July 2007 I became president of the LAUSD School Board; with three new allies we had a majority on the seven-person board. We built a political coalition around changing the status quo and eventually selected a new superintendent. We also increased health-care coverage for cafeteria workers. At that point we were starting to open schools under the new construction program. But we still had not sufficiently changed the vision of what these schools should be and do.

Charter schools had begun to create change models outside of the district's schools. We wanted to create opportunities for schools inside the district to have that kind of flexibility too. In 2006 the president of United Teachers of Los Angeles and the superintendent made an agreement for launching ten pilot schools, called the Belmont Pilots. Today we have forty-eight pilot schools. The pilot program gave school leaders a degree of autonomy over their structure and curriculum and offered parents and young people some choice within the district system.

Then the Great Recession hit California and left children with dramatically less education funding. The superintendent identified where to cut the bureaucracy by almost $3 billion. We cut expenses in central and local district offices by over half. It was intense but we got through it. The most powerful lesson was that people cared and worked together to save public education in Los Angeles.

FROM ZERO TOLERANCE TO ZERO SUSPENSIONS

The next important reform that we implemented was passing the School Climate Bill of Rights in 2013. In the 2007–2008 school year, an incredible 74,765 instructional days were lost to suspensions in LAUSD.[3] The Brother, Son, Selves Coalition, led by young people of color, began challenging harsh zero-tolerance discipline policies. The young people said, "We're getting suspended for every little thing at school, and that needs to change." In response, the board eliminated "willful defiance" as a cause for suspension. It was challenging to move away from suspensions as the first response to behavioral issues, but we did it.

We needed to interrupt the misconception of "If I can't suspend, I'm allowing bad behavior." To the contrary, instead of suspending, you build a relationship with students in which they can learn. We were not going to allow children to be denied education because of an adult's bad day.

Today there are fewer than 5,600 suspensions per year.[4] We didn't change the students. We changed our relationship with the students. And we supported adults in the school differently.

Roughly 485 schools have had training in Tier I Community Building Circles, and approximately 290 schools have had training in Tier II/III Repairing the Harm and Reentry Circles. We have over 250 pupil services and attendance counselors to give more social and emotional support. All schools in the district will be trained in and implementing restorative justice practices by 2020.

People came to see that restorative approaches benefit the school overall. If a campus had fewer discipline issues, that campus had better attendance, better academic achievement, and a healthier budget.

We believe in providing academic and social support to students in a variety of ways, such as by providing health clinics and counselors. Through these services and relationships, we learn about the challenges our young folks face. Personalizing schooling in this way helps us create alternative solutions for students, which is part of restorative justice.

GETTING TO GRADUATION

We implemented A-G for all students as a requirement for graduation in 2016 and have seen positive results. In 2008 LAUSD had a dismal graduation rate of 48 percent; by 2017 our graduation rate had risen to 80 percent.[5] Every student earning a diploma now has completed the coursework required to attend state colleges and universities, and those who pass with a C or better become eligible for admittance.

This is real progress, but no one is satisfied. We now say out loud, "Our goal is 100 percent graduation." We will not make excuses about why we cannot serve all students well. We are at 80 percent. That's still too many students not getting to the finish line. Our movement leaders have worked with LAUSD leadership over the past decade, and we are eager to see investments that increase equity and quality of services across the district.

Many people in nonprofits and among our elected leaders have been involved with us in these reform efforts in LAUSD for over ten years. They need to stay with us despite setbacks. I hear a lot of people saying that an 80 percent graduation rate isn't good enough. I agree with them. But they need to remember that we started at 45 percent, with some schools at 24 percent. We need to continue to remember that systemic change takes a long time, and we must keep pushing!

My purpose for being on the school board is to be of service to this community. As a board member, I can validate community voice. I legitimize the role of community members when they speak at board meetings and make demands. I listen to people when they come with surveys or with petitions, and that creates space for other leaders in the organization to listen as well.

I work closely with my superintendents and LAUSD administrators. But we also create space for authentic, organic community leadership to be part of the discussion. If I hold a budget meeting or a study session on a topic, it includes community members, parents, and young people. I include somebody from the superintendent's office, somebody from SEIU Local 99, and somebody from one of our community partners. In this way I embrace community members as educational leaders.

With leadership comes responsibility. In my formal role as a board member, I hire the superintendent, set policy, approve a budget, and serve as a community voice. I have had to help community members understand my responsibilities in this role. During the Great Recession, I had to explain the budget and ask for support for the horrible cuts we were forced to make. That was hard, but in the end I think it created levels of trust and appropriate levels of partnership.

The relationship that community groups have with my colleagues always has an important influence on the outcome. The community groups pressure the organization in a way that I cannot. They can bring their stakeholders to every meeting. When people from the west side come and talk to their own board member, their influence is completely different from having me talk to that board member. I have to abide by the Brown Act, which says I can ask only two other members for their vote on the initiatives I advocate. But my community allies can ask everybody for their votes.

The fifteen years of work by community groups have been a collection of individual campaigns: the campaign to build a new school in East LA, the campaign for A-G requirements, the campaign for wellness centers, the campaign for breakfast in the classroom, the campaign for ending suspensions for willful defiance. All of these campaigns bring with them new people, dissatisfied customers, and strategic allies, building the capacity for long-term systemic change.

CHANGING THE SYSTEM

For me, education can be a lifesaver. Learning self-efficacy and self-determination is a powerful force for all human beings. Education can interrupt poverty. It enables young people to make different choices about their lives and handle whatever is challenging them at the moment.

Education is the solution to every public policy issue, and in Los Angeles we built a coalition that recognized that possibility through improving educational opportunities in all communities. System change is hard. But we can't underestimate the power of people coming together to do something different.

In the current political climate, everyone who works in education has to double down. We are clear about our purpose when our democracy is threatened and when there is a political discourse of hate and scapegoating. We know that we must rise as a people, and education can play a powerful role in this process. When we get it right, we exhibit the absolute best of humanity, creating learning opportunities for the next generation and creating models of humane, caring, and responsible behavior to pass on.

When I think about an educational justice movement, I think about a strong and healthy society. I think about investments that pay off for everyone. We are talking about investing in ourselves and investing in the pillars of our society in a way that protects our future. Building this movement is about securing our freedom and about building our nation. It is holding the adults responsible to fulfill their role of teaching, learning, and creating more opportunity for all, especially for those who have been left out.

14

WALKING INTO THE COMMUNITY

Community Partnerships as a Catalyst
for Institutional Change in Higher Education

– Maureen D. Gillette –

Seton Hall University, South Orange, New Jersey

Maureen Gillette tells the story of the Grow Your Own Teacher program in Chicago and its role as a catalyst to transform the College of Education at Northeastern Illinois University, where she served as dean. Frustrated that schools of education did not prepare educators to succeed in urban schools, Maureen partnered with community organizations to train parents and community members as teachers in their neighborhood schools. Engaging the staff's active participation, the college transformed itself as faculty redesigned courses and programs to be culturally and politically relevant to urban communities. Faculty now serve as co-learners and co-teachers with community organizers preparing principals, counselors, and teachers to work with families and communities dedicated to quality education and social justice.

> We are already educators and community activists. The only way
> the community is going to get strengthened is if we do it.
>
> —JOSUE CONTRERAS, community-based teacher

I ARRIVED IN CHICAGO in June 2005 to take my first deanship with the College of Education at Northeastern Illinois University (NEIU). As I drove from Paterson, New Jersey, where I spent six years designing and leading the Paterson Teachers for Tomorrow (PT4T) program at William Paterson University, I pondered my goals for the college. At my interview, I described a framework for developing justice-oriented, urban "insiders" who would teach in their home community, act from an ethic of care, and prioritize trust and relationship building with students, families, and community members. The teachers who graduated from PT4T solidified my belief in these insiders. They would serve as a strong cadre of educators focused on student success in schools located in the nation's most economically challenged neighborhoods. As a veteran elementary and middle school teacher, I saw firsthand that when teachers and administrators understand the communities where they teach, build strong relationships with students and families, and know how to access resources from the community, young people flourish.

OUR FIRST STEPS

I began our work by bringing faculty together to discuss priorities and develop a strategic plan. For accreditation we needed a "conceptual framework," or an agreed-upon statement of our beliefs. This document would guide our work, as it would represent collaboratively designed shared values and commitments.

Previously, the College of Education (COE) had focused on developing reflective practitioners creating learning communities. In a series of retreats, the faculty added two critical components: collaboration and transformation. We used a backward design model to describe the characteristics of a COE graduate who could transform their work environment—a school, a district, a community agency, a business—to be just and equitable. Faculty members planned meetings, led colleagues in discussions, and set priorities and action steps. By 2007 we had a theoretical framework and seven strategic goals that served as guides over the ensuing years. Our tagline, which we lived every day, was "COE Professionals: Reflective, Collaborative, Transformative."

ENTER THE COMMUNITY ORGANIZERS:
GROW YOUR OWN TEACHERS

Representatives from the Chicago Learning Campaign, an education reform group made up of leaders from several community groups, called me in 2005. They had obtained legislation and funding to establish the Grow Your Own Teachers Illinois (GYO) program and were developing twelve consortia across the state that included a college of education, a school district, and a community-based organization (CBO). They wanted to recruit, support, graduate, and return "teacher-insiders" to local communities similar to PT4T in New Jersey. But GYO candidates were not traditional college students. They were community members with a commitment to reform in the economically challenged neighborhoods where they lived and in the schools where their children were being educated. It was a brilliant idea, and I enthusiastically signed on.

The COE started with one CBO partner, adding five more over the years. We served three primarily Latino neighborhoods, two African American neighborhoods, and one that is highly ethnically diverse. The demographics of our candidates matched the geographic area where they lived, meeting the goal of recruiting more teachers of color for Chicago Public Schools. Many were bilingual, some came as immigrants, and most were parents who held down jobs while they went to school. GYOers proved to be outstanding learners. Their collective grade point average was 3.2 (on a 4.0 scale). Among them were academic honor society members, McNair Scholars, NEIU's student graduation speaker, and many who graduated with high honors. While at NEIU, they continued to work in schools and communities across Chicago and to speak boldly as equity advocates.

As of 2016, NEIU had graduated fifty-eight fully licensed GYO teachers, forty-one of whom are teaching in "high need" schools. Graduates from the early years have attained tenure, and several serve as cooperating teachers for the next generation of teacher candidates. Some have earned master's degrees. They are leaders in their schools, in the teachers' union, and in CBOs.

BETTER TOGETHER: LEARNING FROM AND WITH EACH OTHER

We know that educator preparation programs must do a better job of preparing aspiring teachers and principals as culturally relevant pedagogues for students of color who live in poverty. Yet most university teachers and principal educators are not people of color and have not been prepared themselves to understand and challenge social structural inequality. Many of our faculty espoused the mission of equity and diversity but were unfamiliar with or uncomfortable in the types of economically challenged neighborhoods where we expected our candidates to work. Rarely in higher education do we engage faculty in critical dialogue about social structural inequality or issues of poverty and the intersections with race, gender, sexuality, language, and culture. Rarely do we ask faculty to examine their own assumptions, beliefs, and stereotypes. The GYO program was a catalyst for me to open that door and walk, with the faculty, into the community to start those conversations.

Change Starts with the Faculty: Community Study Days

One NEIU partner, the Southwest Organizing Project (SWOP), works in Chicago on issues such as immigration, youth engagement, housing justice, and safety. Its education team, composed of SWOP organizers, NEIU staff, P–12 school principals and parents, and GYO candidates, meets regularly to discuss issues pertinent to the neighborhood and its schools. At one meeting, a principal challenged me to bring the faculty into the community to discuss these issues. I did, launching our first Community Study Day. GYO gave me a way to start deep conversations about social justice work with faculty, but this time it would be out of their university zone of comfort.

Our SWOP partners planned the first Community Study Day with GYO students and community members as our teachers. The executive director showed neighborhood foreclosure maps, where staff had placed a red dot on each house in foreclosure. The map was covered in red. The impact was shocking. He noted homes that were abandoned, having become sites for criminal activity or animal infestation. We discussed implications for the local school, which was a linchpin for family and neighborhood stability. He explained how families were moving in with other families so as not to leave the school, exacerbating overcrowding yet providing a sense of security for the children.

COE faculty then worked with parents and teachers on the school's annual school improvement plan. Members of each group sat together, joined by GYO students from the neighborhood who played dual roles as parent mentors and SWOP organizers. It was exciting to watch the sharing of expertise and to see the faces of our faculty as they learned about the outside-of-NEIU lives of our GYO students.

Next we visited the Inner-City Muslim Action Network, a neighborhood agency that organizes around issues such as health, arts and culture, and successful reentry for formerly incarcerated residents. We also heard from faculty at a middle school who had collaborated with SWOP on a grant to build an on-site health clinic. Our day ended with lunch in a locally owned restaurant, joined by partners in the faith-based community. The restaurant owner and the faith-based leader described the importance of their work in the community through a framework of empowerment. Between 2008 and 2016 we held Community Study Days like this one in five partner neighborhoods.

Sharing Expertise in Activism

In 2010 the Illinois State Board of Education raised the passing score on the basic skills test for candidates to enter teacher preparation programs in Illinois. As a result, the statewide pass rate dropped to less than 50 percent, with the pass rate for black and Latino test-takers dropping under 10 percent. This meant that many interested people of color, including some GYO candidates, would face a significant hurdle in becoming teachers.

With our GYO partners, we pushed back against this act: organizers, faculty members, and I met with a civil rights lawyer to consider filing a disparate impact lawsuit; I joined organizers on a trip to the state capitol to convince board of education staffers to change the policy; we helped GYO plan a conference at NEIU to discuss the characteristics of an excellent teacher beyond test scores; and we held a hearing before the Legislative Education Committee in Springfield.

Ultimately, the superintendent refused to roll back the cut score, but we did win a concession. Teacher candidates could submit ACT or SAT scores in lieu of the state test. This lessened the pressure of having to pass one test and provided candidates with an alternative for entry into the profession.

It seemed important that I model the equity advocacy that I expected of the faculty. Over time, more COE faculty members began to speak out on issues of educational equity. They testified before legislative committees, joined activist groups, wrote letters, and developed networks with activist scholars in other parts of the country. Faculty supported Chicago teachers when they went on strike in 2012, supported the Chicago Teachers Union and community groups in fighting school closures, and led a pushback against an unfunded mandate for a statewide student teaching assessment.

Joint Dissemination Efforts

As COE faculty came to appreciate the expertise of our community partners, we moved toward a co-teaching and -learning model. We began to write and present our work together at professional conferences. Faculty members edited a book on GYO that included chapters by organizers, teachers, and researchers. We published articles with organizers and with GYO candidates. These activities assisted faculty in meeting scholarship and service requirements for tenure at NEIU. Further, they provided opportunities for GYOers to gain the "graduate school" cultural capital that demonstrates their professionalism and may propel them into the professoriat.

Awards

I believe that external recognition of our work is important to sustaining it over the long run. Excelencia in Education, the National Association for Multicultural Education, and the American Association for Colleges of Teacher Education recognized the COE for our work, specifically citing GYO as a significant program in developing teachers of color. These awards, in addition to awards received by several of our CBO partners for their advocacy on behalf of their community, encouraged us. Importantly, partners cited them when advocating for resources to support our candidates and the work.

COMMUNITY PARTNERSHIPS AS CATALYSTS FOR INSTITUTIONAL TRANSFORMATION

Over time, our GYO collaborations solidified our focus on social justice and transformational outcomes. But I knew that other changes were necessary. We needed to hire and retain faculty committed to our mission of educating all professionals in solidarity with the community. We had a cadre of experienced faculty who held social justice values when I arrived. But not everyone had experience with or commitment to the type of economically challenged communities that GYO served. Through the Community Study Days, retreats, ongoing focus on mission and vision, and the addition of new faculty members, the transformation of faculty culture became visible in small and large ways. By 2009 job advertisements for new faculty included demonstrated evidence of a commitment to diverse communities as a required qualification. Many faculty members had credentials that could have led to jobs at universities with more prestige, higher pay, and reduced teaching loads, but they came to and stayed at NEIU because of the work.

Our GYO work provided the impetus for the transformation of the COE curriculum. Some faculty members completely revamped the types of readings, course materials, and assessments they used based on learning from the Community Study Days or collaboration with community partners. Faculty members began to select material for courses that could serve two purposes: teach content or strategy and incorporate the lived realities of urban students. For example, after our Community Study Day in a neighborhood with extremely high housing instability, a literacy professor selected an article on P–12 students who experienced homelessness for her class to use in practicing the "close reading" strategy.

Faculty began to make programmatic changes that were influenced by our community work, including completely restructuring the type of general education course work that all teacher candidates received. For example, teacher candidates previously selected from one of three general English courses to fulfill their requirement; now they take one revamped course, "Literature and Literacies," which includes attention to historical and cultural traditions and differences in literature and literacy. The course interrogates dominant Eurocentric modes of thought and examines various literary forms that children experience in different settings, including the community, such as the murals or graffiti found in our partner neighborhoods. As a result, we now expect that teacher candidates will enter their professional sequence with the ability to create lesson plans and units using the community-infused and culturally relevant content knowledge they have gained.

The special education department changed its undergraduate major curriculum to include a new required course titled "Community Partnerships and Advocacy." The course teaches prospective teachers to work collaboratively with peers and community partners to identify needs in Chicago and area communities through service learning projects. Candidates examine key components in the development of effective community partnerships and the cultivation of advocacy/leadership skills on behalf of students with exceptionalities. To pass the course, teacher candidates must provide evidence that they understand the key role that parents and community resources play in the work of teachers, and must demonstrate an ability to collaborate with families and community partners to ensure student success.

NEW DEGREE PROGRAMS: THE MASTER OF
ARTS IN COMMUNITY AND TEACHER LEADERS

The COE embraced the principle of shared expertise across the academy and community. The Educational Inquiry and Curriculum Studies faculty designed a master's degree based on this principle to prepare practitioners to transform schools and communities in more socially just ways. Half of each cohort of students comes from the community, and the other half are practicing teachers. Students take six core courses, designed to be team-taught with community partners so that they can learn from each other's expertise and connect what happens inside and outside of schools. Courses such as "Power, Communities, and Change," and "Digital Literacy: Learning and Leadership," challenge students to develop knowledge and skills to foster reflective, collaborative, and transformative leaders in schools and community settings.

Finally, the COE proved successful in national reaccreditation. I believe this is important, particularly for a college that serves nontraditional students who are often stereotyped regarding their academic ability. In 2012 we met each of the six required standards. In part, thanks to GYO, we received a mark of distinction for our work on the diversity standard.

CONCLUDING THOUGHTS ON TRANSFORMATIONAL CHANGE

Why did NEIU experience a degree of success when some universities gave up on GYO? What will it take to transform the broader universe of schools of education into institutions that partner with and learn from organized communities as part of a larger social justice movement?

Build the Foundation: A Vision for and Commitment to Partnerships

Universities do not typically interrupt or interrogate faculty and administrative perspectives. Institutional leaders must work with community partners to set expectations and develop strategies that empower faculty through learning experiences and significant discussions about justice, equity, and the reproduction of social structural inequality in society and in our educational system. Because of the authentic experiences we structured, faculty embraced the vision and were empowered to create initiatives that transformed the COE. As faculty and administrators, we cannot think that we already know everything about transformational practice, about social justice, about the ways that school and society reproduce social structural inequities, and about our role in building more just and equitable communities. It takes work, and it begins with sometimes difficult conversations.

Joining with like-minded partners for this journey was the next step. When the leaders of the educational institution join with CBOs to create a vision of education in solidarity with the community, amazing things happen. One of the reasons some higher-education institutions gave up on GYO when the work got difficult was because the partnership formation process didn't require buy-in based on a common vision. Community partners did not always clearly articulate their vision, and differences were not analyzed to achieve clarity and consistency in each partner's conception of the work.

Time for Trust and Relationship Building

It is not possible to do difficult, transformational work without trust. Partners must work out differences and support each other. In the beginning of GYO, many hours were spent in face-to-face discussions about what our vision should look like in practice. We held each other accountable and learned together from our mistakes. Without a belief that we were each sincerely working toward the same goal, I could predict that one or the other of the partners would have abandoned the collaboration. The initial trust building takes time but pays so many long-term benefits.

If It's Worth Doing, It's Worth Institutionalizing

Too many innovative educator preparation programs begin with a grant that was designed without collaborative partner involvement. Such programs often operate in niches at the university. It is extremely important to institutionalize programs like GYO so that the structures and benefits are not lost when a grant concludes or funding is jeopardized.

The process of institutionalization underscores the need for buy-in at all levels of the university. As dean, I had to ensure that the upper-level NEIU administration understood how the COE/GYO vision was aligned with the university's mission and vision, and what operationalizing it involved. Throughout GYO's ups and downs, NEIU's administration supported our work with resources and course release time for faculty and staff. In return, GYO graduates became outstanding spokespeople for the university.

I believe that every candidate who aspires to work in schools needs community-based teacher or principal preparation. This includes those who teach and lead in our nation's most challenged communities, as well as those in less diverse, more affluent areas. Unless we all understand the social structural inequality that creates and maintains the conditions found in poor urban and rural communities, and work to build collective responsibility for transformational reform, our democratic system will continue to be in peril.

15

◦-◦-◦-◦-◦-◦-

#SCHOOLISMYHUSTLE

Activist Scholars and a Youth
Movement to Transform Education

– Vajra Watson –
University of California, Davis

The transformation of education is not solely the work of the K–12 school system but demands a new kind of involvement from higher education. Research should not be conducted merely for knowledge production but also in service to social change. Scholar activist Vajra Watson offers a collaborative model that connects the university, schoolhouse, and adjacent neighborhoods. She tells the story of Sacramento Area Youth Speaks, which pairs community-based poet educators with classroom teachers to provide young people with the opportunity to empower themselves through hip-hop, poetry, and performance. Drawing upon the powerful words of young people, Vajra shows what can happen when a university-based researcher reimagines her role and relationship to young people and their communities and schools.

I FOUNDED SACRAMENTO AREA YOUTH SPEAKS (SAYS) in 2008. Over the last decade, SAYS grew from a writing workshop with five students into a movement that reaches and teaches thousands of students each year. Through the training of poet-mentor educators, SAYS is able to bring the community into classrooms, connect the streets and school, and foster connections between neighborhood knowledge and the curriculum. As a result, student attendance has substantially improved, high school graduation rates have increased, and so have students' grades. While these measures are significant, they are not the soul of the story. The essence of SAYS is the unabashed, truth-telling, multilingual voices of young people who are courageously creating spaces that transform lives.

STEP 1: A PARTNERSHIP FOR YOUTH VOICE

Just a couple of weeks after I graduated from Harvard University in 2008, I started at the University of California, Davis, as the director of education partnerships in the School of Education. I soon realized that to ground my work in the needs of the local area, I would have to get out of my office. Since I was new to the region, I spent my first two months meeting with various superintendents, teachers, and school leaders in nearby Sacramento.

In each of these encounters, I heard similar stories about student disengagement from learning. Everyone referenced a literacy crisis across the region: low-income youth of color were not passing the writing portion of the CAHSEE, the California High School Exit Examination. As a former high school teacher and community organizer, and now as a scholar, I wanted to find ways to help the youth of Sacramento succeed.

To strategize about solutions, I held an initial meeting in 2008 and called it a "partnership for youth voice." I invited a wide range of stakeholders, including local community-based organizations, superintendents, district personnel, principals, teachers, and program officers. During the meeting, we broke up into small groups and began thinking across sectors about the ways we were (or were not) supporting students. We used school-based data showing disproportionate success in literacy to guide the conversation and focus our plans.

We came to a jarring realization: we were not working alongside youth to design solutions to student disengagement. In fact, we had not even invited them to this meeting on "youth voice." I realized we were replicating part of the problem: we were leaving them out of the conversation.

Around this time, I was asked to host a table at the annual "Friendraiser" for Youth Speaks in San Francisco. I was on their advisory board, and I decided it might be serendipitous to invite the entire group from the youth voice meeting. My colleague Kindra Montgomery and I provided rides, and we were a bit surprised that most stakeholders decided to attend the meeting, driving two hours each way. It was that drive that led us on a path that would shift youth services in Sacramento.

At the Youth Speaks event, young people's voices filled the room. Spoken-word performance poetry resonated with each of us, and my colleagues were adamant that they wanted something similar for students in Sacramento. By the end of the evening, we made a collective commitment—in word, deed, and resources—to foster spaces for soul-stirring performance poetry.

But how would we do it?

STEP 2: IF YOU'VE GOT SOMETHING TO SAY? *SAYSOMETHING!*

I created a flyer for a writing workshop that would fuse critical literacy and leadership development. I circulated it to my colleagues in the schools and asked them to personally invite their students, particularly their so-called hardest-to-reach youth. I planned for thirty youth to show up. Only five came. At this inaugural meeting, these five students were adamant that they needed an outlet for their pent-up anger and aggression. They pleaded for help, saying, "We're starving for social justice out here, this is not the Bay." In response, I challenged them to seed the solution. I said that I would help them start an organization based on "youth voices for social change." However, to actualize our ideals, they would each need to bring five friends to the next meeting. One month later, fifty-eight students arrived for the writing workshop.

SAYS was born in the hearts of these courageous students who committed themselves to organize one another and lead the way. But not everyone was eager to write. There was one student, Forrest, who sat in the corner and did not want to participate. He had come for the free food and nothing more. I asked him a simple question: *What do you love to do?* He told me that he had dropped out of high school to pursue his art. This young white kid, with his punkish style and skateboard, loved to draw. I asked him to create a logo for SAYS. By the end of our second meeting, Forrest had drawn the logo that we still use on all of our materials.

From that moment onward, SAYS started growing exponentially. More than one hundred students attended each of the community-based writing workshops. We decided to hold these sessions at the Sierra Health Foundation, free of charge. This venue is spacious, and the setting, perched on the Sacramento River, is stunning. Students would eat delicious meals on the deck and watch the sunset. Although this detail might seem unimportant, it was critical to participation and morale. A student told me at one of the very first gatherings, "I know you love us." "How do you know that?" I retorted. "Because of the food!" A community began to form. These middle and high school students who were struggling in school began to feel comfortable with one another and themselves. They started to own the space, not just occupy it.

Because the sessions were growing so rapidly, we started using a microphone and sound system to accompany the writing workshop and open mic. Music became another significant cultural cue that demarcated this youth setting. For instance, a grand piano sat in the foyer of the foundation. When SAYS first started, nobody touched the piano. After a few sessions, students began playing the piano while their friends beat-boxed and rapped during one of our many impromptu hip-hop sessions. When the foundation would close, we did not want to leave. On some nights, we would stay in the parking lot, conversing for hours.

The students were engaged and committed to SAYS, but most of them were uninterested in school. As a former high school teacher, I was dismayed that their grades were dangerously low while their intelligence was so high. We began to have serious conversations about education. "Why should I care about school?" a student argued with me. "School does not care about me!"

STEP 3: IT IS NOT A CRIME TO BE WHO YOU ARE

Although the writing workshop still focused on spoken-word poetry, I added another element that focused on educational justice. I believed that to fully address *root problems*, we must *seed solutions*. That's what we tried to do. For example, in one session, I devised a lesson based on a slogan by the antiapartheid activist Steve Biko. I asked the students this question and developed a series of prompts to accompany it: "What is the greatest weapon in the hands of the oppressor?" Toward the end of the class, I provided Biko's answer: "The most potent weapon in the hands of the oppressor is the mind of the oppressed."[1] At the end of each writing circle and dialogue, students stepped to the mic to share their spoken-word performance poetry pieces, which were personal, political, and educational.

A provocative piece by Mercy Lagaaia is layered with creative criticism and rhetorical reasoning. She draws important parallels between schools and prisons and challenges teachers to accept students in their entirety and encourage them academically, emotionally, and culturally. She recites, "Yo board of education! Why we so bored of education? . . . It seems like every time a colored kid pulls up, a disorder is being ordered and our education seems to be the cost of all this trauma. . . . I know I'm smart, but I was taught to never forget where I came from. So for you to see the good in me, best believe you gon' see the hood in me. . . . School and prison are the same language and I'm all too fluent. . . . So tomorrow will just be another day of prison, I mean school."

STEP 4: SCHOOL IS MY HUSTLE

During the winter and spring of 2009, the youth and I met on a regular basis. On many occasions, the writing workshops ended late, and I needed to drive students home. Each time I met with families, a pattern emerged that I found disconcerting. To my dismay, parents expressed a genuine disbelief that a program from UC Davis took an interest in their children. In subsequent conversations, I learned that none of the students or their families had ever visited the university, even though it was less than thirty miles away. UC Davis, as an ivory tower, simply felt out of their reach and beyond their worldview.

Only a narrow causeway divides the college town of Davis and Sacramento, the capital of California. The space between this top-tier research university and its adjacent city is not just physical but ideological, racial, and economic. Two-thirds of residents in Davis are white, while Sacramento is heralded as the tenth most diverse city in the US. The average family income in Davis is $134,000, compared to $33,000 in Del Paso Heights in Sacramento, where the SAYS Center is located.[2] We may witness the same sunset, but our horizons are viscerally different.

Based on my burgeoning partnership with schools, my close relationship with the Sierra Health Foundation, and a newfound ally in the college's student affairs office, I was able to secure seed funding to bring 350 disenfranchised youth to UC Davis from 8 a.m. to 10 p.m. for the first annual SAYS Summit College Day. These students had a 1.5 or lower GPA and/or consistent disciplinary problems at school. We held it in May 2009, when SAYS was just five months old. The theme was "School Is My Hustle."

Although we geared the summit toward youth, it seemed to have the greatest impact on teachers. I received a barrage of phone calls that night and over the weekend from educators who told me they needed SAYS in their classrooms, immediately. They saw their students come alive through this form of literacy. Eventually, the dedication and persistence of these classroom teachers brought SAYS into schools across the district from 2010 onward.

Student feedback from the SAYS Summit College Day at UC Davis included the following: "I felt free today. That never happens to me. Thank you so much." and "SAYS is really powerful. It makes me want to be somebody and make a change in my community, society, world. I love the vibe."

STEP 5: WRITE TO LIVE

To meet the demand from local teachers to bring SAYS into schools, I went back to my research on community-based educators and realized we had a unique opportunity at UC Davis to bring the community into classrooms. Blending together a grassroots community and youth organizing framework, my colleague Amaya Noguera and I developed a training program that would prepare nontraditional educators from the neighborhood to work alongside classroom teachers.

Now in its ninth year, each cohort of community educators partakes in a six-week training program in three core areas: critical pedagogy, social justice youth development, and literary arts. Once the course sequence is completed, the participants can be hired as part-time university employees at eighteen dollars per hour. Over the years, we have trained more than thirty poet-mentor educators who are all people of color ranging in age from eighteen to fifty-plus. They represent a unique mix of community activists, hip-hop MCs, and spoken-word artists. The majority grew up in the Sacramento region and attended schools in the area; some even dropped out of the very schools in which they now work.

According to SAYS coordinator Patrice Hill, "Some of us are facilitating workshops at the same schools that expelled us. . . . We are these young people! We sat in the same classrooms, went through the same experiences! . . . It's a lifelong commitment to the uplifting and empowerment of our babies. This calling is indeed the pedagogy of our lives."

SAYS hires poet-mentor educators because of their poetic prowess and neighborhood knowledge. Inside their classrooms, inquisitive sharing circles and radical writing activities move students' narratives into the center of instruction. As a result, decrepit, depressing, under-resourced classrooms become radiated with a light of love for learning.

One high school teacher offered this feedback:

> OMG, to quote my kids. First class with poet-mentor educators. One of my two MOST difficult classes, the one that's caused me more times than once this year to question (seriously) this profession. WOW! Every single one of them is enthralled. The quiet kids. The disruptive kids. The followers. The leaders. All of them. And they're asking about when are you coming back again, how can I get involved with SAYS. WOW!

STEP 6: #SAYS4LIFE

SAYS provides a platform for a new dimension of public scholarship as students present their ideas to a wide range of audiences, from their peers to policy makers and from school superintendents to university academics. The students' insights serve as a call to action—or, as we say, a "poetic service announcement."

Over the last decade, a single seed has grown into a forest. SAYS began with five students and now works intensely with hundreds of students in five school districts throughout Northern California every year. SAYS has provided an opportunity for young people to become *the authors of their own lives and agents of change.*

Asani Shakur (aka Geno) is just one example of the transformative power of SAYS. I met Asani in 2012 when he was coming home after serving a seven-year prison sentence. He was unable to return to Richmond, California, because of a court-ordered stay-away. I was told by a colleague that he had a powerful message for the youth, and he soon started working for SAYS. He took a hiatus to go to UCLA, but now he is back in Sacramento and working at UC Davis. As he reflects upon his journey, he finds an outlet through poetry. He writes:

What do you see when you look at me?
Young Black male with tattoos?

He must have felonies.
While this might be partially true, you are only seeing from one side of view.
Yes, I moved weight to get my muscle.
Then I met Vajra and she taught me that school is my hustle.
A Black rose that grew from the Richmond concrete.
Neglected from the sun and the water.
A product of the mis-education system.
A product of the school-to-prison pipeline.
I returned home to SAYS
Now look at me.
I graduated the top of my class—straight A's—from a top tier university!
En route for my law degree
These are my damaged petals.
Tell me what you see?
    —ASANI SHAKUR

SAYS itself has also flourished and grown in many ways. The SAYS Summit College Day now serves a thousand middle and high school students each May; we have a robust curriculum for our in-class residencies and after-school programs; we oversee an internship program for UC Davis undergraduates to work alongside poet-mentor educators in the community/schools; we organize Sacramento's Youth Poet Laureate competition and MC Olympics; and we recently received funding from the City of Sacramento and AT&T to address youth violence through our intensive mentoring initiative called Project HEAL—Health, Education, Activism, and Leadership.

STEP 7: WARRIOR SCHOLARS

In her book *Decolonizing Educational Research*, Leigh Patel challenges us to consider "whether an entity borne of and beholden to coloniality could somehow wrest itself free of this genealogy."[3] Applying this to SAYS, I wrestle with the ways that education—or more specifically, the school site—is both the doorway into social control as well as the window out of it. Since learning can literally mean the difference between life and death, between a dorm room and a prison cell, how do we reimagine and embody education as the praxis of freedom?

In Paulo Freire's seminal text, *Pedagogy of the Oppressed*, he asserts that critical literacy is a vital component of self-actualization and agency. "Human beings," he writes, "are not built in silence, but in word, in work, in action-reflection."[4] As a collective, we seek to embody the vision of Sacramento Area Youth Speaks. SAYS stands on the side of equity, social justice, and democracy. Our life's work is in service to this struggle—a struggle that is real but also really beautiful.

> *Our legacy is louder than the ivory tower*
> *Older than borders that divided us into being something we are not*
> *Somehow we forgot*
> *To put tongue in rightful place*
> *Use words to transform space*
> *So hear we be*
> *From privilege and poverty*
> *Accepting no praise or pity*
> *Just mouth-full of poetry*
> *Centered in space*
> *Speaking between the past and this place*
> *Future*
> *Calling us forward*
> *For inside us*
> *Lives the next generation*
> *Now choose*
> *Genocide or education?*
> —VAJRA WATSON

PART FOUR

INTERSECTIONAL ORGANIZING

Linking Social Movements to Educational Justice

16

⊸-○-○-○-○-○-⊸

JANITORS ARE PARENTS TOO!
Promoting Parent Advocacy in the Labor Movement

– Aida Cardenas –

Building Skills Partnership

AND

– Janna Shadduck-Hernández –

UCLA Center for Labor Research and Education, Los Angeles

Many service workers in Los Angeles are immigrants who came to this country so that their children could get a good education, yet they attend some of the district's lowest-performing schools. Aida Cardenas and Janna Shadduck-Hernández tell the story of how the janitors' union came to take on education advocacy. They opened a "parent university" offering workshops to help janitor parents support their children's education and advocate for improvements in the system. They negotiated time and resources in contracts for parents to take workshops at the job site and also help to engage their fellow parents and their children. Aida and Janna end with a call for all unions to learn from this example and support working parents and the cause of educational justice.

AIDA'S STORY

I am the daughter of Mexican immigrants and the granddaughter of braceros, contracted laborers who worked in mines during this country's labor shortage in the 1940s and 1950s. I am the first in my family to graduate from college, receiving a BA in history from UCLA in 1996, with a specialization in labor and workplace studies. Coming from a hardworking immigrant family, I wanted to understand their history and learn about the labor conditions that low-wage workers have experienced in this country over generations. I became an activist for labor and immigration rights at

UCLA and in my community, and soon after, I was recruited as an organizer with the Justice for Janitors campaign. For the last twenty years, I have directed educational, leadership, and organizing initiatives with janitors and other low-wage service workers. And for the last ten years, I have led the Building Skills Partnership, a unique training collaboration between the janitors' union, responsible businesses, and the community to advance the skills and opportunities of low-wage building service workers and their families across California.

JANNA'S STORY

Raised in an Upstate New York immigrant household, I grew up speaking several languages and going to school with the children of immigrants who had secure full-time jobs in local businesses, factories, and public institutions. By the time I graduated from high school in 1982, however, most of these factories and large businesses had relocated or shut down, forcing the families I knew to move, reskill, and find new jobs. Deindustrialization forced schools to consolidate and close too. This transformation from thriving manufacturing town to a place of boarded-up factories and high unemployment had a great impact on me. When I went to college, I focused my studies on community-labor relations, immigration, and education to better understand the economic changes I had witnessed. I learned about the Justice for Janitors campaign in Los Angeles and felt inspired that workers did not have to be victims but could organize in this new economy. I moved to LA in 2002 to use my degree and research skills to help advance workers' rights. As a labor educator and researcher at the UCLA Labor Center, I have participated in documenting the union's innovative and bold strategies to organize low-wage immigrant janitorial workers. I serve proudly on the board of the Building Skills Partnership to advocate for educational access and justice for janitors and their children.

JUSTICE FOR JANITORS AND THEIR CHILDREN, BY AIDA AND JANNA

Janitors in Los Angeles are not just workers; they are parents who care deeply about their children's future and the quality of the education they receive. Many are immigrants who came to this country precisely so their children could get a good education and improve their lives.

In 2006 the union representing janitors and office cleaners, Service Employees International Union–United Service Workers West (SEIU–USWW), partnered with the UCLA Labor Center and the UCLA Institute for Democracy, Education, and Access to survey hundreds of janitors in the Los Angeles area. We found that janitors identified educational access for their children as the most important issue outside of their collective bargaining agreement—more important to them than affordable housing, health-care reform, or immigration reform. The survey also showed that three-quarters of all janitors expected their children to go college. After all, that is what their fight for job stability was about. The survey also showed that workers strongly believed that their union should get involved in matters of educational access and reform.

As janitor parents looked at school data with researchers and union leaders, however, they found that the schools their children attended were some of the lowest-performing schools in the district in terms of high school completion rates and college preparation. In many of these high schools, less than half of students graduated, and few met the admissions requirements for state colleges.

The union leadership's mandate was clear. In 2008 SEIU–USWW named as one of its top priorities improving equal educational opportunities for workers' children. It joined with the Building Skills Partnership (BSP) to launch the Parent Worker Project as a series of initiatives that began with the establishment of a Parent University. This "university" offered workshops to janitor parents to help them better support their children's learning and advocate for improvement in the quality of education offered. Building the knowledge and skills of janitor parents would lay the foundation for a range of efforts to close the gap between family dreams and the realities in their children's schools.

Founded in 2007 by a cohort of committed partners, BSP's mission is to improve the quality of life for low-wage service workers and their families by increasing their skills, access to education, and opportunities for career and community advancement. The partnership includes more than forty-five janitorial companies, thirty-five building owners, the Building Owner Managers Association of Greater LA, SEIU–USWW, community organizations, and educational institutions, including the UCLA Labor

Center. BSP now trains over forty-two hundred California service workers, including janitor parents, in vocational and life skills.

The Justice for Janitors Campaign

Janitors are the hidden labor force that makes Los Angeles work. While most office workers sleep, thousands of janitors work hard in the shadows of the night cleaning skyscrapers for some of the world's largest corporations. Almost three-quarters of janitors are women, and many are heads of household. Most janitors are Latino/a immigrants living in low-income communities, and their children attend some of the most under-resourced public schools in the city.

Janitors have a special history in Los Angeles. The groundbreaking Justice for Janitors (J4J) campaign, launched in Los Angeles in 1990, transformed the city's landscape, putting low-wage immigrant employees at the forefront of new workplace and social movement organizing. In April 2000, janitors across the city went on strike and won the hearts of the people of Los Angeles. This three-week strike brought the janitors and their labor conditions out of the shadows. Their mops and brooms, held in clenched fists, became the symbol that SEIU–USWW used to demand dignity, respect, just wages, and benefits for hardworking service workers.

The Parent Worker Project

Through the J4J campaign, many janitors gained experience engaging in collective workplace action and winning campaigns. These experiences equipped janitors with important skills to advocate and make demands not only for their own children's educational success but also for district-wide reform. Research shows that union parents are more likely than other parents to get involved in their children's schools because of their labor and community-organizing experiences.[1]

Janitor parents nevertheless needed new skills and much greater knowledge of the educational system if they were going to be successful advocates in this complex arena. The Parent University curriculum was developed organically in response to parent worker needs. The curriculum covers a wide range of topics, from how to read a report card, to parents' rights, to how to participate on a school site council. Workshops discuss ways that parents can be engaged in schools and provide much-needed information on issues such as course requirements for admission to California state colleges, scholarships and financial aid, creating a learning environment at home, and the rights and opportunities of immigrant students.

The California School-Family Partnership Act allows parents, grandparents, and guardians to take time off from work to participate in their children's school or child-care activities. Since most janitors begin their shifts at around 6 p.m., they need to take time off to participate in events such as back-to-school night, parent conferences, assemblies, and other after-school activities. Union leaders requested that this right be explicitly stated in their 2008 collective bargaining agreement. This contract stipulation made more janitors aware of their right to take time off to attend school activities and facilitated its enforcement in the workplace.

The Parent University model promotes a worker-to-worker approach to adult learning. In partnership with the UCLA Labor Center and other community-based organizations, janitor parents are trained to deliver workshops in their workplace, at their union hall, or in their children's school. During the summer months, some parent leaders take a leave from their janitorial job, and their wages are covered by BSP or SEIU–USWW. This gives them the opportunity to deeply engage in "train the trainer" programs and events, develop leadership skills, and reach out to other parent workers like themselves. While on leave, parent leaders work full-time surveying their peers, analyzing data, developing worker-centered curricula or information sheets, and becoming trained worker leaders within their respective workplaces, schools, and union. Parent leaders provide information sessions during lunchtime in the same skyscrapers where they work. These sessions often take place at 10 or 11 p.m. in lunchrooms or break spaces where janitors converge.

Janitor parents also coordinate field trips and cultural activities to connect other janitors and their children to extensive city resources such as museums, universities, zoos, aquariums, and state parks. While riding the bus to the activity, parent leaders conduct short sessions with parents about the public education system, how to voice their interests and concerns at their children's schools, and how to foster meaningful partnerships to improve their children's education. Workers collaboratively identify their needs and priorities in these spaces with the goal of engaging other janitor parents to become involved in school activities and to ultimately become committed advocates for quality education reform.

Offering sessions at worksites can minimize many of the obstacles to parent engagement, such as transportation, child care, and job commitments. Most traditional parent programs take place after school or in community spaces that are geared toward parents who do not work or who work part-time and have more flexibility. These programs are generally not accessible to custodial workers who have set schedules and work the night shift. The Parent Worker Project is the first program of its kind to address the education system where organized janitors spend most of their time, at work or in a familiar and trusted space like their union hall.

Snapshots of Janitor Parent Leaders

Marcia Gomez has been a janitor at the Wells Fargo Tower in downtown Los Angeles for twenty-three years and has been a participant in our summer Parent Leader Program since 2014. She is a mother of a twelfth-grade high school student, a second-year college student, and a son who is a graduate of Westwood Aviation Technical College. As a single mother, Marcia guided her three children into successful career and college pathways on her own, so she understands firsthand the importance of parent participation in the success of her children's education. Because of her participation in union activities and with BSP, her children have been able to secure financial aid to attend community college to study mechanics and early childhood development. Marcia wants to model the importance of education, so she enrolled in BSP's vocational ESL (English as a second language) program, and became a US citizen through the citizenship program. Marcia continues to provide workshops to other parents and encourages them to be active participants in their children's education.

Amparo Gonzales became a parent leader participant in 2014 after being inspired by her own participation in the Parent University workshops. A mother of four boys, she had long felt confused about how the massive LA school district operated. The workshops helped her navigate the educational system and support her son so he could attend Pasadena City College and Humboldt State University. Her third son attends Downtown Magnets High School, and her youngest is finishing middle school. Amparo has worked as a janitor and been a member of SEIU–USWW for fifteen years. Like Marcia, Amparo continues to share her story with other parent workers. She believes it is important to be engaged as a parent so that she can model this kind of participation to other parents and their children.

Janitor parent leaders like Marcia and Amparo are working with BSP and UCLA trainers and educators to build a parent cohort to advocate collectively for educational improvements. Worker family priorities include quality classrooms with qualified teachers, increased high school completion rates, and accessible pathways for the children of workers to go on to higher education.

In the Parent University curriculum, educators break down the complex structural and education problems faced by families in low-income neighborhoods and stress the importance of building strong relationships and networks among worker parents, their children, their schools, and the educators at their union and workplace. BSP understands that when parents are engaged, schools and the community form a partnership to enable quality, culturally responsive, and respectful learning environments. We know that when parents and community educators work in partnership, schools perform better, community resources are maximized and shared, and students are motivated and improve academically.

Working with Youth

As we began to work with parents, we learned that janitors' kids in middle school and high school often have limited resources at their schools to prepare or help them excel in STEAM fields (science, technology, engineering, art, and mathematics) or navigate access to the higher-education system. So we began to offer workshops for school-age children, often holding them at the same time parents are taking ESL classes or a parent leadership workshop. A robust and creative curriculum offers young people hands-on opportunities to learn about science by making toothpaste, building model volcanoes, learning about weather cycles, and much more. For high school students, BSP offers workshops on applying for college and financial aid, writing personal statements, budgeting for the first year in college, and immigrant student rights and resources.

On any given Saturday at the union hall, you will see younger kids playing a fun memory game about the life cycle of plants or building a structure out of straws and pipe cleaners to learn about architecture, construction, and urban space. In another room, a group of high school students will be writing their personal college essays and learning about the college application process and scholarship opportunities. BSP has also incorporated a youth internship component to its summer programming, in which the children of janitors support BSP program coordination and work with other youth and shadow trainers so they can learn to conduct workshops or science lessons themselves.

Lessons Learned and Challenges Ahead

BSP and SEIU–USWW are committed to engaging worker parents in their children's education with the goal of creating pathways out of poverty. It is a model for the country in which employers, unions, workers, and schools partner to promote academic success for all students. Janitor parents want to support other worker parents and their children to succeed. In their capacity as leaders and parent advocates, janitor parents feel valued by their union and their employers when they are recognized as parent advocates.

This educational model faces challenges similar to other parent engagement programs. Worker parents are often tired and stretched for time, and many have other family commitments that can impact participation. Working the night shift is not easy. For a program like this to be successful, permanent nonprofit staff need to support the coordination of program development to solidify a strong cadre of parent leaders.

We found that parents were much more comfortable meeting at the union hall instead of their children's school. Janitor parents don't trust or feel as comfortable at schools compared to their more familiar workplace or union office. In future stages of the project, we will be developing strategic and more expanded relationships with key schools where janitor children attend.

CONCLUSION

Low-wage parent workers have a stake in equity-minded public school reform. They are deeply committed to seeing their children succeed in their adopted home. The union parent members in this project understand that the success of the next generation is in their hands. The Justice for Janitors campaign was a landmark labor organizing effort that shifted the narrative of passive low-wage immigrant workers to one where workers have agency and are leaders in their workplaces and unions, demanding just working conditions and labor contracts. The workplace power of janitor parents can help create an educational justice campaign that seeks to improve access for working-class children. Many working parents and union members are already engaging in school improvement efforts on their own, but it is also critical to create innovative programs and negotiate collective bargaining agreements that increase knowledge, opportunities, and access for parents to participate in their child's education.

It is time for all unions to support working parents to become school-based activists who can collectively achieve equitable education with a social justice agenda for all learners. Creating a national network of educational justice organizations based on the model of the Building Skills Partnership is a promising strategy toward change. This is especially urgent today, as our public education system is under attack. Mobilizing equity-minded working parents is essential to counter the corporate takeover of our public schools. Janitor parents are calling on their unions, employers, school districts, and other workers to reimagine a society where every school, no matter what neighborhood it is in, can and must be a quality public school.

¡Si se puede!

17

--o-o-o-o-o-o--

THE SAME STRUGGLE

Immigrant Rights and Educational Justice

– José Calderón –

Pitzer College and Latino/a Roundtable
of the San Gabriel and Pomona Valleys, Pomona, California

José Calderón describes how he has made the connection between the struggles for immigrant rights and educational justice in his work as an activist scholar in the city of Pomona, in Los Angeles County. José begins by telling his own story of arriving as an immigrant to this country and the role of public education in opening opportunities in his life. He discusses a number of overlapping campaigns: ending police checkpoints, fighting for voting rights, creating alternatives to gang violence, and promoting community schools. He discusses the deep relationship-building processes that occurred through these campaigns that created multiracial coalitions with a united vision combining immigrant rights and educational justice.

MY PASSION FOR BUILDING BRIDGES between the struggles of our immigrant communities and educational justice lies in my own history as an immigrant. I came to the US at the age of seven with my parents, who worked in the fields as farmworkers all their lives. We lived in the barrio above a gas station in one room with a wood stove and no indoor plumbing. I started school with seven other students from Mexico who, like me, could not speak English. We all faced the dual problem of being poor and unable to speak English. Thanks to a teacher who stayed with me after school, I was able to learn English and find some success that led to my graduation from high school, from college, and ultimately from a doctoral program.

The other Mexican-origin students in my class were not as fortunate; all of them eventually dropped out of school.

When I graduated from the University of Colorado in 1971, I took a bus to Delano, California, in order to meet Cesar Chavez and join the farmworkers movement. When I arrived during a grape workers strike, I heard the words that changed the rest of my life. At an evening rally at Forty Acres, the central headquarters of the United Farm Workers Union, Cesar challenged the young students there. He told us that there is only one thing for sure, and that is death. Between now and when you die, the question is how we will use our lives. We can easily throw it away on drugs, selfishness, and material things, thinking these will bring us happiness. But he assured us that if we commit our lives in service to others, to empower others, when we grow old and look back on our lives, we will be able to say that they have truly been meaningful.

Transformed by this experience, I returned to my hometown of Ault, Colorado, and created a school with eighteen young English language learners in an old garage in my parents' backyard. When the local school board told our students to go "back to Mexico" if we wanted bilingual education in the schools, thirty students and I organized a four-day, seventy-mile march to the state capitol. Hundreds of supporters met us along the way and cheered us on. When my students returned, they took the lead in organizing schools throughout the county, resulting in some of the best bilingual programs in the state.

Because most of the English language learners came from immigrant families, the issues of educational justice in the schools became intertwined with the struggle for immigrant rights in our communities. Hence, some of the same parents who organized for bilingual education in the schools also organized to protect undocumented residents. They won a commitment from Sheriff Richard Martinez and the Weld County Sheriff's Department that they would not actively stop and detain undocumented immigrants. These experiences led me to make a fourteen-year commitment to organizing in Northern Colorado for both immigrant rights and educational justice.

I left Colorado to pursue a PhD in sociology at UCLA, but it was through these community organizing experiences that I truly came to understand the connections between the inequities in our communities and the problems that underrepresented students face in the classroom. My struggles with learning English and growing up in a poor immigrant farmworker family laid the foundation for the connections that I ultimately came to make, as a graduate student and professor, between immigrant and education rights issues and led me to become an activist scholar. As an activist, I have been part of efforts to build coalitions between parents, teachers, students, and community-based organizations to organize for both immigrant rights and educational justice. As a scholar, I conduct community-based research in support of these organizing efforts. As an activist scholar, I combine research and organizing to create change within the schools and in the neighborhoods where parents and students reside.

Fighting English-Only in Monterey Park

An early example of connecting the movements for immigrant rights and educational justice occurred in the city of Monterey Park, where I resided with my family while completing my sociology doctoral degree. Monterey Park, located just east of Los Angeles, is a city with over sixty-two thousand residents. It has gone from being 85 percent white in 1960, to being a majority-minority city today. According to the US Census, in 2015 about 65 percent of the population was Asian Pacific, 30 percent was Latino, and just 4 percent of the population was white.[1] Many members of the Asian Pacific community and almost all the Latinos are immigrants.

I worked with other organizers in Monterey Park to build trust between community partners and researchers as a basis for making social change. Too often, researchers have gone into a community simply to gather their research and then leave when it is completed. Trust building takes longer. It requires that community partners see researchers contribute to community efforts, then embrace the research as a tool to advance their goals. In my case, I combined the roles of researcher and organizer and built trust by making a long-term commitment to the Monterey Park community.

In 1986 Monterey Park's all-white city council passed a resolution requiring English-only in city literature and public signs. I was part of the Coalition for Harmony in Monterey Park (CHAMP), a multiethnic group of residents that brought together immigrant parents from the Latino and Asian Pacific communities to defeat the ordinance and eventually vote out of office its main proponents. Later, in response to right-wing politicians and individuals who blamed the Chinese community for street congestion and overbuilding in Monterey Park, our coalition elected candidates who called for planned development without casting the issue of growth in anti-immigrant terms.

This coalition created a level of trust that also helped solve conflicts in the city's schools. When racial tensions erupted between Latino and Asian Pacific students in the Alhambra School District, immigrant parents worked together to create a district-wide Multi-Ethnic Task Force comprising parents, students, PTA members, the teachers union, staff, and administrative personnel. To counter the claims of some school officials who denied the existence of racial tensions in the schools—blaming tensions on "machismo" or the natural "hormones" of teenagers—I worked with the task force to carry out a survey of fifteen hundred students, including three hundred limited-English-speaking students. We found that 86 percent of the students perceived racial tensions as a very serious problem in the schools. We used the research to get the school board to adopt a policy for dealing with hate-motivated behavior, to institutionalize classes in conflict resolution, and to create the option of mediation as an alternative to student expulsions.

We knew that conflicts in the schools and the community are linked. As a large influx of Asian Pacific immigrants, primarily Chinese, had settled in Monterey Park, the unity with Latino parents and students was brought about by finding common ground rooted in their histories as immigrants. By advancing a strategy of coalition building, the two groups were able to collectively use research as a tool to advance a multicultural curriculum and conflict resolution programs that benefited both groups.

The experience in Monterey Park helped to solve a dilemma that I faced in connecting my position in the academic world with community-based participatory research, teaching, and learning. Rather than perpetuating the traditional idea that researchers should not participate in the organizations they study, this participatory research and action experience allowed for my involvement as both an organizer and researcher in the community. When I accepted a faculty position at Pitzer College and moved to the Pomona Valley in Los Angeles County, I took the lessons learned in Monterey Park and began organizing in the city of Pomona. Here again, I combined research and organizing to help parents and students build connections between the immigrant rights and educational justice movements.

Ending Police Checkpoints in Pomona

My students and I first joined parents and community leaders in organizing a broad-based coalition to build a local social justice movement that exposed the unjust use of police checkpoints to target immigrants. Over the past twenty-five years, the city of Pomona has experienced the demographic changes taking place throughout Southern California. According to the US Census, it is now a majority-minority city that in 2015 was about 71 percent Latino, 6 percent black, 9 percent Asian Pacific, and 11 percent non-Hispanic white.[2] When the police in the city of Pomona began to locate checkpoints in front of schools and businesses and in neighborhoods that primarily served Latino families and immigrant workers, immigrant parents and supporters formed a coalition called Pomona Habla (Pomona Speaks). Through this coalition, we launched a research project that spurred organized actions against traffic checkpoints in the city of Pomona. Our research uncovered data that showed that fewer than .001 percent of the drivers being stopped at checkpoints were driving under the influence of alcohol.[3] The statistics also showed that the majority being stopped were undocumented immigrants who did not have a driver's license and could not afford to pay the exorbitant ticket, towing, and impoundment fees.

The Pomona Habla coalition launched a series of demonstrations and actions in which community people and students held signs alerting drivers to the checkpoints on the streets. Tensions in the city peaked when the police held a four-way checkpoint (covering four street corners) involving police from forty cities, resulting in the stopping of 4,027 vehicles, the impoundment of 152 of them, and the issuing of 172 tickets.[4] In response, Pomona Habla led a demonstration of more than a thousand people and stationed students and community members at every checkpoint. The research and actions resulted in the city council's agreeing to stop four-way checkpoints, to allow checkpoints only in residential areas, and to develop an ad hoc committee to review citizen complaints and recommendations.

The community-based research and organizing of this coalition became a model for the passage of ordinances in San Francisco, Los Angeles, and Baldwin Park that permit an unlicensed driver to allow another licensed driver to take custody of the vehicle rather than having it impounded. These statewide efforts led to the introduction of a bill by California assemblyman Gil Cedillo, which was signed into law by Governor Jerry Brown in 2011, that restricts local police from impounding cars at a traffic checkpoint simply because a driver is unlicensed. This ultimately led to the passage of a bill allowing undocumented immigrants to obtain driver's licenses. Pomona Habla, which included community-based organizations as well as students from local schools and colleges (including students from my classes at Pitzer College), gathered more than ten thousand signatures in the region in support of this bill.

ORGANIZING AND RESEARCH IN VOTING RIGHTS

In reaction to these victories, the Pomona Police Association, together with other conservative forces in the city, targeted one of the leaders of this coalition, city councilwoman Cristina Carrizosa. They tried to oust her from office by placing a bill, Measure T, on the ballot in November 2012 to replace the election of city council members by district with at-large elections. The measure sought to turn back the will of the people in Pomona who, following lawsuits by the Mexican American Legal Defense and Education Fund and the Southwest Voter Registration Project, voted in 1990 to scrap citywide elections in favor of single-member districts to bolster minority representation. Working with the coalition, my students and I carried out research that revealed a voting rights history of how the district elections came about and who was behind Measure T. Our research exposed how the police association had given over fifty thousand dollars to back this bill and uncovered their sponsorship of a leaflet depicting a white hand extended upward over brown hands reaching from below.[5] A multiracial coalition of community members and organizations held a press conference, walked door-to-door, and on Election Day defeated Measure T, meanwhile helping elect two additional council members who were supportive of immigrant rights.

COALITION BUILDING ON STREET VIOLENCE

After the defeat of Measure T, the issue of "gangs" and street violence emerged in the city. In response to a growing homicide rate, the police carried out a raid of alleged gang members that resulted in the arrests of 165 people. Our coalition believed that the most successful strategies for dealing with growing violence among youth needed to focus on prevention rather than criminalization and enforcement. My students and I, along with members of a progressive coalition led by the Latino and Latina Roundtable and the United Food and Commercial Workers Local 1428, carried out research for a series of community meetings. We argued that gang violence would not exist if gangs did not satisfy the desperate needs of young people for family, education, mentoring, housing, employment, health care, and spiritual and social support. As we expanded the coalition to include parents, students, teachers, and community-based organizations, we championed a strategy of countering "gangs" with an economic justice plan and capacity-building strategies for quality jobs, housing, health, education, and preschool/after-school programs, particularly in low-income sectors of the community.

In this process, we studied successful gang-prevention models, including one developed by Father Gregory Boyle in Los Angeles. This model addresses young people's needs by developing an alternative elementary school, after-school and daycare programs, community organizing, and an extensive Homeboy Industries economic development project, including Homeboy Bakery, Homeboy Silkscreen, and Homeboy/Homegirl Merchandise. We convened a community summit conference based on this model to advance the idea of addressing the structural problems affecting young people and their families in Pomona.

ADVANCING COMMUNITY SCHOOLS AND A BROADER MOVEMENT

This new direction in addressing youth issues led to the development of a partnership between the community-based Latino and Latina Roundtable organization, of which I am president, the Pomona Valley Chapter of the NAACP, and the Pomona Unified School District. As part of this partnership, a community development committee has held monthly meetings to implement various community building and educational transformation projects. This coalition has included parent leaders from the community-based initiatives on checkpoints and gangs. It pursued the proposals first identified at the summit meetings to shift away from law enforcement and toward strategies focused on youth and community development.

The coalition has started to implement the community schools concept, where schools provide education and health and social services to children, parents, and community members. After the Latino and Latina Roundtable and the NAACP spoke in favor of a resolution to implement the concept of community schools, the Pomona Unified School Board unanimously voted its support. Pomona Unified advanced strategic plans that include (1) culturally relevant and engaging curricula; (2) an emphasis on high-quality teaching, not high-stakes testing; (3) support systems that include health care and social/emotional services; (4) positive discipline practices, such as restorative justice; (5) parent and community engagement; and (6) inclusive school leadership committed to making the transformational community school strategy integral to the school's mandate and functioning.

Following Cesar Chavez's principle of using one's life in service to others, I helped get the school district to join a coalition that has organized an annual Cesar Chavez Pilgrimage march and festival focusing on social justice themes. These themes, including solidarity with Black Lives Matter and with Mexican students gone missing in 2014 and supporting ethnic studies and sanctuary for all, offer examples of the broad-based understanding we have developed about the connections across the issues of educational justice and immigrant rights.

With this intersectional understanding, the partnership has implemented workshops for hundreds of students and parents in how to qualify for the Deferred Action for Childhood Arrivals (DACA) program, how to obtain a Matricula Consular card (an official identification document issued by the Mexican government), and how to obtain a California driver's license. More recently, as part of a College for All statewide coalition, this partnership has expanded to endorse and actively implement California State Senate Bill 1050 (whose passage was led by one of my former students, Senate president pro tempore Kevin de León) to create a kindergarten-to-college pipeline of educational opportunity and success for students from low-income, English language learner, and foster youth backgrounds. The partnership on these pipeline issues has led to a series of extraordinary developments, including educational workshops for hundreds of parents, many of whom then lobby with us at the state capitol for bills to provide safe schools for immigrant children and to ban the use of public funds to aid federal agents in deportation actions, as well as other legislation to protect vulnerable students and advance educational equity.

CONCLUSION: EDUCATIONAL JUSTICE
AT THE HEART OF IMMIGRANT RIGHTS

My own life experience and trajectory show how the pursuit of education is fundamental to the immigrant struggle. I am an organizer, an educator, and a member of the community. I use community-based research and organizing to build bridges across immigrant communities and between the immigrant rights and educational justice movements. This type of engagement and research shows the intimate connection between the two. It emphasizes the systemic and structural aspects of inequality and involves activist scholars in working alongside excluded communities on common projects to tackle the root causes of racism, exclusion, scapegoating, and inequality in our educational system and in our communities.

Scholar activists build a foundation of trust with communities by making a long-term commitment to working in genuine partnership to find and implement solutions to the problems communities are facing. This type of action and research moves away from charity or service and toward creating new models of democratic participation and coalition building for social change. This intersectional model appreciates the structural foundations of inequities experienced by immigrant communities in the classroom and community and builds strategies that connect the struggles for educational justice and immigrant rights.

18

───○─○─○─○─○─○───

ORGANIZING INTERSECTIONALLY
Trans and Queer Youth Fighting for Racial and Gender Justice

– Geoffrey Winder –

Genders and Sexualities Alliance Network,
Oakland, California

The most powerful way to create movements that intersect and overlap is to ground them in the young people who are living the struggles. For Geoffrey Winder, that means centering the most vulnerable voices in our communities, especially those of LGBTQ youth of color. The Genders and Sexualities Alliance (formerly the Gay-Straight Alliance) Network supports these and other youth in over four thousand GSA clubs, where young people organize on issues such as ending zero-tolerance discipline and, perhaps surprisingly, anti-bullying policies that turn out to harm LGBTQ students of color. Geoffrey describes the challenges of creating a truly inclusive movement and the possibilities for change as the next generation of trans and queer youth step forward as social justice warriors.

I FIRST BECAME INVOLVED WITH LGBTQ issues when I was sixteen and attending high school in Davis, California. I came out at age fifteen, and I was the only out student at my school. It was the late 1990s, and the level of awareness and public acceptance of LGBTQ issues was still just beginning. There were very few TV shows about LGBTQ people, and the internet barely existed. *Will and Grace* first aired in 1998, the same year that Matthew Shepard was murdered in a brutal, antigay hate crime.

I identify as a queer, multiracial person of color. I am African American and Korean, and also gay. I grew up as an interracial and transnational adoptee in a suburban, predominantly white college town. Needless to say,

I've had an intense and intimate relationship with the concept of intersectionality for a long time.

Like many LGBTQ youth, I started a Gay-Straight Alliance (GSA) club at my school because I wanted to feel less alone. I was looking for a sense of community, a place where I would fit in. Even though we were just a few members at the beginning, I realized that we could do more than just meet and talk about our lives. We could actually try to make the school better for LGBTQ youth. At first, we were just trying to make people realize that LGBTQ students go to this school. We also organized campaigns like the Day of Silence, in which people wouldn't speak for an entire day as a demonstration of how people are silenced in their identities.

Soon after starting my club, I joined a newly formed national organization called the GSA Network, which supported student clubs like mine. The GSA Network, which in 2016 changed its name to Genders and Sexualities Alliance Network, uses an organizing model, so they helped us carry out campaigns like the Day of Silence. The network also opened us up to the wider world of LGBTQ issues and organizing. I was one of hundreds, now thousands, of students who are following a similar path, starting or joining a GSA club.

ONE SCHOOL, ONE COMMUNITY, ONE GENERATION AT A TIME

The work of GSA clubs is the work of public school integration. We view our work as being in the tradition of the Little Rock Nine and other black students who first integrated public schools. We use GSA clubs to force schools open and integrate education systems that weren't designed for us and are actively hostile to us.

The GSA Network supports students to start GSA clubs, which are extracurricular student-based support and advocacy groups for LGBTQ issues. Student leaders run these clubs that advocate for justice and attempt to change hearts and minds in environments that are often openly hostile and dangerous. A GSA club often starts as a support group for members to talk about who they are, as mine did; then it becomes a social group where students have fun together; and then it becomes an activist group where students contemplate how to make things better for all LGBTQ students. Most clubs are involved with all three goals at different times through the year. The GSA Network especially supports the activist clubs to run campaigns or lead broader social change efforts in their schools or communities.

As a next-generation trans and queer youth leadership organization, we help build the leadership and strengthen the identity of LGBTQ youth. We give them the skills they need to be leaders in their school clubs as well as in broader social justice movements and the world.

We also believe in generational change, meaning we are invested in seeing young people grow up and go to school with LGBTQ youth who are out and proud leaders with a healthy sense of identity. We have a long-term strategy of achieving LGBTQ people's normalization and equalization and liberation in society. We believe that the existence of a GSA club changes the nature and fabric of a school community. To change a school is to change the local community, and to change the local community is to change the larger society, one generation at a time.

ZERO TOLERANCE—FOR LGBTQ YOUTH

After graduating from Davis High School I joined the board of the GSA Network while I attended New York University. I joined the staff in 2008 and started the organization's racial and economic justice program in 2011. Meanwhile, GSA clubs, which had started in the late 1980s and took off in the mid- to late 1990s, were forming in all parts of the country by the mid-2000s. But we noticed two trends: (1) GSA clubs were typically formed in predominantly white, suburban, and well-funded schools; and (2) in more diverse schools, even when youth of color joined the GSA, they were gone by the end of the school year.

We realized that a new system had been put in place since I had been in high school—the school-to-prison pipeline—and it was in full swing by 2011. Zero-tolerance policies had proliferated and been incorporated into every school regulation, pushing out LGBTQ students of color. Schools singled out LGBTQ youth of color, taking them out of the regular school system and putting them into what were often called "continuation schools," a kind of alternative school for at-risk youth. While harsh discipline affects all students of color, there are some particular ways in which zero-tolerance and punitive policies work together to make public schools uniquely challenging for LGBTQ youth.

These policies too often mean zero tolerance for an LGBTQ student or zero tolerance for the expression of that student's identity. Some teachers punish or suspend students for "willful defiance" when they question a teacher's bias against LGBTQ people or voice a different view in favor of LGBTQ rights. Zero-tolerance dress-code policies penalize trans and gender-nonconforming students for expressing their gender identity.

Many people think that zero-tolerance anti-bullying policies should help LGBTQ students, but the opposite is true. These policies create a one-size-fits-all solution for any sort of code infraction. It's like mandatory sentencing: teachers and administrators don't have any options that take into account what may have gone on before an incident happened. When an LGBTQ youth gets in trouble for a bullying incident, it's usually not because they bullied someone else. It's because they've been bullied over the course of months or years, and they finally have had enough, so they fight back and are disciplined for doing so. Even putting your hands up to defend your face from being hit could be considered fighting under a zero-tolerance discipline code. In many cases the punishment for the student who's being bullied is disproportionate to what the student did; they're often suspended, expelled, or transferred to a different school. These kinds of hostile environments make students drop out. Under this punitive approach, both the LGBTQ youth and the student who bullied them get the same punishment, usually suspension, which often makes things worse.

Zero-tolerance approaches to bullying don't give students or the school a chance to repair the harm or to create a new, positive, and supportive school environment in which these things don't happen. The restorative justice approach that we advocate gets at the underlying root bias and addresses it. Students and staff hold restorative justice circles, where participants share their perspectives, listen to one another, identify the harm committed, and work to resolve issues. Through this process, the LGBTQ youth feels safer, heard, and that others understand their identity matters; hopefully the young person either wins a new ally or at least no longer has somebody who's actively hostile to them.

As part of a restorative justice response, some GSA clubs have the student who bullied attend GSA meetings or go with the LGBTQ youth around the school to observe how other students treat them. Through this process, both students benefit and the school community at large is made better. The climate of the school is improved overall.

EXPANDING UNDERSTANDING— INTERSECTIONALITY AND SOLIDARITY

In 2009 and 2010 a series of highly publicized bullying-related suicides of LGBTQ students appeared in the media. In late 2010 the Obama administration issued a letter instructing all school districts to adopt a policy of zero tolerance for bullying. Adult LGBTQ rights groups seized on this as a victory for youth. But the GSA Network feared that this blanket approach would undermine the work of student organizing and educational justice advocates like us, and might actually harm LGBTQ students.

The GSA Network pushed other groups in the LGBTQ movement who advocated for anti-bullying policies with the best intentions to instead advocate for restorative justice approaches that protected LGBTQ youth. We worked to shift the national narrative away from punitive, zero-tolerance discipline approaches and toward pro-LGBTQ restorative justice approaches.

The GSA Network also has spent years working with different groups in the educational justice movement, particularly the Alliance for Educational Justice, the Dignity in Schools Campaign, and the Advancement Project. In the beginning, not all groups understood how our issues connected to the work they had been doing. Six years later I am confident that most of the groups have embraced intersectionality and could explain how the issues of LGBTQ youth connect to schools and to educational justice.

The GSA Network partnered with the Advancement Project to publish a policy brief advocating against zero-tolerance anti-bullying policies and to support the school-to-prison-pipeline action camps the group sponsored. The camps brought together hundreds of youth and parents who were organizing against zero-tolerance school discipline across the country. We worked closely with the Alliance for Educational Justice and other groups in these camps to shift the understanding and practice of the movement in regard to LGBTQ issues. We spent a year training folks on the issues that impacted LGBTQ youth in schools, not only bullying but how school discipline policies and dress-code policies affected the lives of LGBTQ youth of color. Our work resonated with educational justice folks, who knew how inherent bias by a teacher or administrator could create discriminatory outcomes. They came to understand the connection between the issues that LGBTQ youth face as well as how punitive and zero-tolerance approaches hurt them.

Young people were involved in all of the work to engage with the broader educational justice movement. Youth build solidarity much more quickly than the adults. It probably took twice as long for the adults to figure out how and why we were working together as it did for the young people.

The GSA Network builds relationships through interactive workshops with different groups, as in the action camps mentioned earlier. We meet people in person and explain what the issues are and how they connect. We also show up and commit to the work that we are doing together. We participate in the Dignity in Schools Campaign Week of Action, for example, and we work with the Alliance for Educational Justice on their #EndWarOnYouth campaign. We don't just lift up our issues and leave.

We didn't create real solidarity within a year or two. It happened in year three, four, and five when LGBTQ youth started to become naturally included and were no longer an afterthought.

When we engage the larger education reform movement to address the issues facing LGBTQ youth, many older folks find it challenging because it's very different from their lived experience. Part of intersectionality requires being in solidarity even when it isn't your direct life experience. You need to be able to understand the ways systems work simultaneously on multiple identities or be empathetic enough to understand why a group of people is looking for a solution to a problem and accept their truths on the issues that are most critical to them, even if they aren't your own.

Creating an inclusive movement is challenging because authentic and true solidarity is hard to come by. Adults working with youth, white folks working with people of color, straight folks working with queer folks, cisgender folks working with trans folks—it is hard to walk in someone else's shoes or imagine your life as someone else's. It is even harder to learn to share what little power or access we may have accumulated for ourselves to further someone else's struggle. The level of solidarity that's needed to create truly inclusive movements takes time to build, and as adults we often feel like we don't have time.

True solidarity can also come from the accumulated experiences of living, playing, and going to school with people who are different and being able to recognize our common humanity and struggle from an early age. This is the world young people in the educational justice movement are creating.

THE ISSUES ARE SO SIMILAR—WHAT ABOUT THE SOLUTIONS?

At some point in my years of talking with the Alliance for Educational Justice and the Dignity in Schools Campaign about the issues that LGBTQ students faced, we had a common realization. We were discussing how LGBTQ youth of color exist at the least protected, least supported, most vulnerable position in terms of oppressive systems and access to power and privilege. When we examine their lives, we can see that multiple systems are failing them: the education system, the foster system, the homeless youth system, and the juvenile justice system. Patriarchy, capitalism, and white supremacy all place trans and queer youth on the losing end, contributing to challenges in every aspect of navigating the world.

Then we realized that we were talking about the same systems in each of our own groups, and in many cases the same youth. It turned out that many of the educational justice and racial justice groups had LGBTQ youth in their memberships, in their leaderships even, but they didn't regularly, actively, and openly address that aspect of their identity.

In both LGBTQ communities and communities of color, LGBTQ youth of color are our most vulnerable students. All of the systemic issues facing youth of color are exacerbated for LGBTQ youth of color; the same goes for institutionalized bias against LGBTQ youth. So how do we approach systems change in a way that supports those who are the most marginalized or for whom the most systems intersect? What are solutions that address all of these systems at once? We believe that if we operate from the most marginalized, the solutions we create will benefit everyone. In other words, a school that fully supports a black trans woman can support any student regardless of their identity. That's intersectional organizing.

Ending the use of suspensions for behavior that is judged subjectively, such as "willful defiance" or "disruptive behavior," and therefore the most affected by bias, is a multi-issue, intersectional campaign. This kind of bias is deeply rooted in systems of white supremacy, patriarchy, and class oppression. A black trans student would benefit from ending a policy that relies on subjective and biased judgments, but so would students of color, trans students of all racial identities, and many other students.

In addition to changing anti-bullying and punitive school discipline policies, we also work to address the funding inequities in schools. One of the biggest barriers to GSA clubs in underserved or low-income communities of color is the lack of funding to support any extracurricular activities at all, as well as any mental health or social services that students, particularly LGBTQ youth of color, may need. So GSA clubs in California worked with other educational justice groups to change how schools are funded. The new funding formula that we helped win allocates more funding for schools that have more students in high-need populations.

When GSA clubs advocate for the needs of LGBTQ youth, it leads students to think about the bigger picture of funding in their schools. Most recently, GSA clubs called upon the California state government to declare all schools sanctuary schools that would protect students from all forms of violence. These are both examples of how intersectional organizing benefits all students.

NEXT GENERATIONS OF LGBTQ ORGANIZING

The organizing by young LGBTQ people over the last twenty years has been fundamental to the societal shift that we've seen. We've had almost twenty years of students going to public school with LGBTQ students who are out and proud. We've seen the visibility of LGBTQ people skyrocket in terms of mainstream acceptance. The current generation saw the legal recognition of gay and lesbian marriage, and we have seen a level of acceptance for LGBTQ people that I never imagined was in the realm of possibility when I was starting my GSA club.

The next challenge this new generation of LGBTQ youth activists faces is destabilizing the rigid gender binary that underpins our culture's toxic patriarchy and the normalization of trans and gender-nonconforming individuals in the American psyche. Just as the previous generation fought for the cause of lesbian, gay, and bisexual people, this new generation is up for the fight for this new frontier!

For me, being a member of my GSA club changed my life. It gave me a sense of purpose and a sense of struggle and community. There's something exciting about working with LGBTQ youth, because they are always the fiercest of the youth social justice warriors. They are building a movement at the intersections, with solutions that are intersectional, because their lives are at the intersections.

I'm excited for the new generation of LGBTQ youth and youth of color to be the leaders of this world. LGBTQ young people are forming the backbone of the resistance movements across the country. They've gone to school with all different types of people, and they are far more tolerant of diversity. We're seeing much larger numbers of the younger generation identifying as LGBTQ. A majority of these LGBTQ youth are youth of color, with many more avenues for identity and self-expression than in the past.

LGBTQ youth activists today experience the world as young people with intersecting and multilayered identities. They develop complex analyses to explain the world around them, and their visions for liberation and justice are bold and far-reaching. The solutions they invent, whether through new technology or organizing strategies, are just so creative and relevant in their ambition and hopefulness.

EDUCATIONAL JUSTICE AS A CATALYST FOR A NEW SOCIAL MOVEMENT

– Mark R. Warren –

THE STRUGGLE FOR EDUCATIONAL JUSTICE entered a new era with the resurgence of the white supremacist movement during the Trump administration. This right-wing movement threatens a wholesale attack on our communities and on many of the gains of the movement we worked so hard to win. There is a new urgency and a new energy for social movements to support one another and resist these attacks. The educational justice movement is poised at the center of these storms. Given the centrality of the struggle for the right to education in the history of American democracy and civil rights, the educational justice movement promises to be a catalyst to galvanize a broader movement that unites the issues and communities struggling for racial, economic, and social justice.

Despite the new urgency, our struggle for educational justice precedes the Trump era. The latest phase of this movement came together during the eight years of the Obama administration. That administration's more assertive efforts to enforce civil rights law and its openness to challenging harsh and racially discriminatory school discipline practices opened up opportunities for the educational justice movement. However, the administration also continued federal policies to enforce high-stakes testing and support the privatization movement by encouraging school closings in black and brown communities and the expansion of charter schools.

The truth is that profound racial inequities and injustice in public education far predate the Trump and Obama administrations. They are rooted in deep-seated systems of white supremacy in the United States. The struggle for educational justice, therefore, is part of a long-term historic struggle for freedom and liberation. We are at a new moment and must respond to new challenges, but the success of the current struggle involves building on and strengthening the work of the past.

In this concluding essay, I highlight important lessons for movement building that are featured in this book. At the end, I emphasize the need to expand efforts at cross-movement and intersectional organizing. These are my thoughts in my words, but they draw from and incorporate the insights and collective wisdom offered by the movement builders in these essays and beyond.

CHALLENGING DEEP-SEATED AND SYSTEMIC RACISM

The educational justice movement must explicitly challenge racism and call for solutions that address racial inequities. Many Americans, especially white Americans, cling to the notion that public education represents a path for children of color to access the American Dream. They hold up individual success stories and applaud the hard work that created achievement. Yet the essays in this volume show that individual successes remain the exception to the rule. The harsh reality is that public education is part of a larger system that systematically denies opportunity to youth of color and keeps their communities without power.

Challenging racism in education requires challenging the entire system of white supremacy. The assaults on public education are part of larger assaults on black and brown communities, including gentrification that pushes people out of their homes and communities, and policing practices and deportation procedures that incarcerate black and brown people. Jitu Brown puts it bluntly: "Black people are just not valued. This is not just about education. This is about a belief system that hates black people."

In the educational justice movement of the 1990s and early 2000s, many groups, often those led by white organizers, did not name racism. They were not necessarily blind to racism, but they believed calling it out was divisive, would alienate potential supporters, and could be counterproductive to winning gains. Perhaps there was also an implicit belief that with the end of legal segregation it was possible to make gains without addressing racism directly.

The tide has now turned decisively. People of color have moved into greater leadership of the movement and are speaking truth to power. Parents and youth of color are angry about the treatment they have received at the hands of the educational establishment and often by teachers and school staff. Many of the African American leaders who have contributed to this volume, such as Jitu Brown and Zakiya Sankara-Jabar, highlight the depth of antiblack racism in the United States. Pam Martinez and others address deep-seated racism toward Latinos, focusing on Chicanos and Mexicanos, whose oppression is rooted in the conquest of Mexican lands in the Southwest. The new phase of the movement is closely tied to the historic struggles for freedom and racial justice in black and brown communities.

Black Lives Matter and the broader movement it represents have also strengthened the resolve of the educational justice to target racism. Black Lives Matter has militantly confronted the country with the extent of violence and brutality that continues to be directed toward black people. It has unleashed a new wave of activists and allies within and outside communities of color that overlap with educational justice movement builders. When youth organizers in the Alliance for Educational Justice call to #EndWarOnYouth, they align the messages of the movements for black lives and for educational justice.

In this new era targeting racial disparities turns out to be an effective strategy for winning policy changes. Highlighting racial disparities in school discipline, for example, and emphasizing the injustices of zero tolerance as it targets black and brown children, pushed districts like Denver and Los Angeles to change policy and moved state legislatures in places like Colorado to pass new legislation.

Challenges remain. Even as the tide has turned against zero tolerance, and the number of suspensions has fallen markedly in many districts, the racial disparities in suspension rates have not budged: black students are still three times more likely to be suspended than white students. Our movement has to redouble its efforts to target racial inequities; we won't return to the days of pretending that racism does not lie at the heart of educational injustice.

BUILDING ALLIANCES LED BY COMMUNITIES OF COLOR

People who are the most impacted by injustice—meaning young people and their parents and families in low-income communities of color—must lead the educational justice movement. Many families are deeply angry about the racism they experience in the educational system and beyond. There is a power to the stories of Zakiya Sankara-Jabar, Glorya Wornum, Carlos Rojas, Christina Powell, Joyce Parker, and others in this book that no advocate speaking for youth and parents of color can match. These stories bring urgency and moral force to the demand for change.

When people speak up for themselves, they are no longer simply victims of an unjust system. They become leaders capable of mobilizing their communities to pressure institutions to change. And they have knowledge, skills, and values that make essential contributions to the pursuit of equity and justice in education.

It is long and hard work to build participation and leadership among parents and young people of color in some of our toughest communities. People who have been oppressed by poverty and racism suffer from trauma and many other challenges, yet they also bring wisdom and strength from their struggles for survival. The essays in this book shine a light on successful organizing models to build participation and leadership in communities of color—from Los Angeles to Denver, from Chicago to the Mississippi Delta, and from New York to Boston. These models embody the exciting work of healing, transformation, and liberation.

We have seen the power that can be generated by diverse alliances that bring parents and youth leaders together with legal advocates, scholar activists, and other allies. But professional advocates who have better education, greater resources, and more political connections often dominate national alliances compared to low-income parents and students. The organizers and leaders in these essays have worked hard to keep parents and young people at the forefront of the educational justice movement. Indeed, Joyce Parker in Mississippi reminds us that "there can be no national without the local," meaning that strong national movements rely on a wide and deep base of organized people in local communities. Participation by parents and young people keep the movement grounded in and accountable to the needs of those most impacted by injustice.

Indeed, powerful national movements link and reinforce local struggles rather than simply target the federal government. The romance of leveraging power in Washington blinds many advocates to the reality that people live in local communities where institutions play decisive roles in their lives. Despite the increasing influence of the federal government over public education, primary decision making for schooling remains at the local level. The national movement needs to strengthen local struggles, not suck the energy and resources up and away from them.

Jitu Brown in Chicago describes how #FightForDyett represents an emerging model for broad alliances based on self-determination by communities of color. African American parents and young people in Bronzeville set the course for the hunger strike, while national actors provided critical support to this self-determined struggle. Meanwhile, the local struggle was "nationalized," and its victory then inspired activists across the country and helped build a national movement against school closing.

We now face the challenge of broadening the movement to be more inclusive and united. Carlos Rojas and Glorya Wornum challenge adultism and call for intergenerational models where adults and youth work side by side yet center young people and their voices. Maisie Chin speaks to the need for intentional processes that create strong forms of black and brown unity in the face of forces set to "divide and conquer" communities. We need efforts to engage with Native communities as well as the many Asian American communities that are struggling for educational justice within deep-seated systems of racial oppression.

CREATING A VISION FOR EDUCATION

The educational justice movement needs a vision and program for the kind of education communities deserve. Students have the right to well-resourced, high quality, humane, and culturally relevant education that addresses students' holistic needs and empowers students and families.

The educational justice movement may be better known for what it is against than what it is for. We are against high-stakes testing that cripples our young people's education; massive school closings in black and brown communities; privatization that shrinks public education and expands privately run charter schools that lack public accountability; harsh and racially inequitable school discipline policies, the regular presence of police in schools, the criminalization of our youth, and the violence committed against young people in schools and communities; the systematic underfunding of public education in low-income communities of color; the low standards of education, the narrow curriculum, and the "drill and kill" teaching practices that alienate our children from learning; and the dehumanization of children and parents of color through routine practices that exclude and bully them.

Campaigns to oppose these policies and practices typically involve calls for positive approaches to education reform: supporting schools rather than closing them, increasing funding to public education rather than cutting it, and providing support to students rather than disciplining them. But it is often easier to bring people together and out onto the streets to oppose a threat rather than dig in for the long, hard work of creating, winning, and implementing positive programs. In the long run, though, people stay committed to social movements because they believe in a vision of a better, more socially just society. Movements succeed when they galvanize people behind these kinds of visions as well as their concrete embodiment in practical programs of change.

The educational justice movement has begun to do serious visioning work. In the essays in this book, there are many inspiring examples of building a more positive future:

- a program in New York City to open more than one hundred community schools that are rooted in community and family engagement and that address the social, emotional, and health needs of students and their families;
- the Bronzeville community's initiative to create the Walter Dyett Global Leadership and Green Technology High School to prepare black youth to be full participants in the global economy and civic life of the future;
- efforts across the country to create restorative justice programs as a strategy for deep cultural change in schools, to provide social and emotional support to students, to create a safe and supportive environment for all students, including LGBTQ youth of color, and

to create humane relationships between school staff, students, and their families;

- efforts to develop culturally relevant curricula starting at the pre-K level and featuring hip-hop literacy in high school;
- "justice reinvestment" efforts to shift resources away from the criminalization of youth and into supporting schools and communities; and
- youth organizing groups that create student-centered and empowering learning environments where young people heal from trauma, develop critical thinking and leadership skills, and organize to fight for issues they care about.

The challenge before us is to knit these initiatives and programs into an integrated and compelling vision and program. Several groups are working in this direction. The Journey for Justice Alliance and the Alliance to Reclaim Our Schools, for example, have put forward visions for community schools that include many of these positive features. The task goes beyond listing demands. It is an organizing and movement-building challenge: how to unite the various components of the educational justice movement so that people create and embrace the larger program even as they dig in and focus on their own piece.

UNITING EDUCATORS AND FAMILIES OF COLOR

The educational justice movement must find ways to bring educators together with families of color. Parents, youth, and community organizers can push for change from the outside, but creating new models of empowering education will require the work of educators on the inside as well. It is one thing to change policy but another to change the actual practice of educators in schools.

In these essays, we see echoes of the profound mistrust that often exists between families of color and educators. When Glorya Wornum questioned the racial bias in the history she was taught in Boston, teachers called her "disruptive" and sent her out of the classroom. When Zakiya Sankara-Jabar declares, "I can't make a teacher love my son," she questions whether white teachers truly care about black and brown children. Black and brown families are angry about the racist treatment that children and their parents routinely receive at the hands of educators. Meanwhile, teachers' unions for too long have been obstacles to demands for change arising from communities of color. Opposition from teachers' unions stalled early organizing victories at combating zero-tolerance discipline in Denver and Los Angeles. There are deep-seated issues of care, compassion, stereotyping, and power that must be addressed.

There is potential for change. By building power for families and communities of color, movements confront racist practices and change power relationships. We see this happening as national teachers' unions, joined by a small but growing number of local unions, are shifting away from advocating zero-tolerance discipline and moving toward supporting parent and youth organizing efforts and their demands for restorative alternatives. In the face of the privatization movement, unions are coming to see their interests aligned more and more with grassroots organizing efforts. Many have banded together in the Alliance to Reclaim Our Schools and are working to create meaningful partnerships where power is shared. The Chicago Teachers Union provides a model of what a strong alliance between the labor and racial justice movements can achieve even against powerful odds.

By exposing injustice and creating a moral force, social justice movements also change hearts and minds. The vast majority of educators enter the teaching profession because they care about children and want to help them grow and develop. This does not make them immune from racism, but it does provide a basis for human and moral connection. As Sally Lee and E. M. Eisen-Markowitz show, when we appeal to educators' sense of justice, demonstrate alternative approaches that work, engage their participation in the process, and provide them with the necessary supports, they can be a force for deep cultural change in schools. This kind of change happens when teachers build new relationships with empowered parents and young people that directly confront racist attitudes and practices in schools and communities.

In addition to the work of Teachers Unite in New York, we have learned about several other cases of educators who collaborate with organizing efforts rooted in communities of color, including pre-K teacher Roberta

Udoh. Padres & Jóvenes Unidos now partners with its former adversary, the Denver Classroom Teachers Association, to implement restorative justice in schools across the district.

These partnerships are not limited to K–12 schools. We have seen how school board members like Mónica García in Los Angeles can create systemic changes district-wide when working in alliance with community and labor organizations. Higher-education leaders like Maureen Gillette are transforming teacher preparation through partnerships with communities. Scholars like Vajra Watson are engaging with young people, schools, and communities through exciting hip-hop literacy and empowerment programs, creating new models for scholars to be activists in an educational justice movement.

BUILDING A HUMANE MOVEMENT

The struggle for educational justice is ultimately a struggle for our humanity. If we want our schools to be humane, caring, restorative, democratic, and empowering communities, then our movement needs to reflect these values. Indeed, since our dominant society falls far short of these ideals, the movement is a crucible for building these new kinds of relationships, indeed to prefigure the society we are working to create. Building this kind of countercultural space within a society that is structured by racial violence and profound inequalities as well as individualism and consumerism is no easy task. And the movement has to nurture this caring culture even while it is also hard-hitting, strategic, and focused on making change in the real world of power politics.

Many of the essays in this book point to where we can start to create a culture of care: by building upon values that have been sustained in communities of color through years of oppression. Jitu Brown speaks to the care and commitment of black parents who put their lives on the line in a hunger strike to save their community school for its children. Maisie Chin asks how educators can love children yet hate their parents and shows how black and brown parents are the ones calling forth the "better angels" in our schools. Although it takes time and effort, Geoffrey Winder shows how true solidarity can be created across the lines of difference within the movement by building upon the deep empathy that comes from experiences of racial oppression. Youth are often the first to welcome diversity and lead the building of inclusive spaces. Carlos Rojas and Glorya Wornum tell adults to learn from young people who are the best at creating spaces that are fun, supportive, and feel like home. In the end, if we do not create communities that are better, more humane and inclusive than what people experience in schools and in the dominant society, we cannot build and sustain our movement and ourselves.

INTERSECTIONAL AND CROSS-MOVEMENT ORGANIZING

Educational justice cannot be achieved within schools alone but must be connected to broader efforts to address poverty, immigration status, and the other issues that affect children's lives. We have seen that public education works as part of a larger system that keeps communities of color poor and lacking power. Fighting for educational justice, then, is a key part of building power for young people, families, and communities.

Movements for economic justice, decriminalization, immigration reform, affordable housing, environmental justice, and LGBTQ rights seek to build this kind of power as well. Yet for the most part these movements continue to operate in their own domains. The essays in this book offer exciting models for cross-movement organizing by creating alliances with labor, immigrant rights, racial justice, and LGBTQ rights movements. The challenge is to make these alliances the norm rather than the exception.

There is a new urgency to movements connecting and supporting one another in the current political era. The rise of conservative and white supremacist forces threatens all progressive movements, from black lives and public education to the rights of undocumented people and women's reproductive rights. If we do not win together, we will lose on our own.

Some of the voices in this book challenge us to go beyond cross-movement organizing to think and act intersectionally, meaning to develop analysis and strategy based on how systems of oppression intersect in the lives of the most marginalized people. If we focus on the threats to immigrant children, we will recognize that immigrant rights and educational justice are, in the words of José Calderón, "the same struggle." Meanwhile, LGBTQ youth of color, as Geoffrey Winder argues, are at the forefront of both educational justice and LGBTQ movements, because intersecting systems subject them to marginalization in multiple ways. Kate McDonough and Christina Powell show that when girls and gender-nonconforming youth of color assert their voices, they create "schools girls deserve." These schools and strategies that create safe spaces for queer girls of color are likely to be humane and supportive for all students.

The educational justice movement itself lies at the intersection of racial and social justice in this country. Educational justice centers the lives of youth of color in low-income communities who are at the epicenter of interlocking systems of injustice, from education to criminal justice, and from the economy to public health. Black youth have the highest rates of poverty and incarceration of any group and are the most likely to live in communities suffering from violence, police brutality, and environmental degradation. As Jonathan Stith shows, systematic state violence amounts to a "war on youth" that targets black youth with particular vengeance—on the streets *and* in schools.

Breaking these systems through an educational justice movement unlocks the larger struggle for social justice for all. Gains in education will impact almost every other sector, including the economy and democracy itself. Indeed, the future of social justice lies in the hands of the next generation. The nature of the education they receive inside schools, in their families and communities, and in the movement itself, plays a critical role in determining the future. Will young people be cogs in a machine, fodder for prison, or warriors for social justice?

The fight for educational justice begins where each of us stands. If we act together, we have the chance of a lifetime to move our country off its course of racial oppression and toward a society based on justice and humanity. We create this kind of society when we build a movement that fosters the free and full development of all of our young people, their families, and their communities.

ABOUT THE CONTRIBUTORS

JITU BROWN is a community organizer for the Kenwood Oakland Community Organization in Chicago. He is cofounder and national director of the Journey for Justice Alliance.

JOSÉ CALDERÓN is professor emeritus of sociology and Chicano/a-Latino/a Studies at Pitzer College in Claremont, California. He is also president of the Latino/a Roundtable of the San Gabriel Valley and Pomona Valley in Los Angeles County.

NATASHA CAPERS is a parent organizer and the coordinator of the Coalition for Educational Justice in New York City. She is a graduate of New York City public schools and is the mother of two children.

AIDA CARDENAS is executive director of the Building Skills Partnership based in Los Angeles. She previously served as an organizer for the Justice for Janitors campaign.

MAISIE CHIN is cofounder and executive director of CADRE (Community Asset Development Redefining Education) in South Los Angeles. She was a founder and national leader of the Dignity in Schools Campaign.

ELANA "E. M." EISEN-MARKOWITZ is a high school teacher in New York City and a member of the board of directors of Teachers Unite.

MÓNICA GARCÍA is president of the board of education for the Los Angeles Unified School District.

MAUREEN D. GILLETTE is dean of the College of Education and Human Services at Seton Hall University in South Orange, New Jersey. She is the former dean of the College of Education at Northeastern Illinois University in Chicago.

DAVID GOODMAN is an independent journalist and author, a contributing writer for *Mother Jones*, and the host of the public affairs radio show *The Vermont Conversation*.

BRANDON JOHNSON is an organizer for the Chicago Teachers Union. He is a former middle school teacher.

SALLY LEE is founder and executive director of Teachers Unite in New York City. She is a former public school teacher and former cochair of the Dignity in Schools Campaign.

PAM MARTINEZ is cofounder and codirector of Padres & Jóvenes Unidos (Parents and Youth United) in Denver, Colorado.

KATE MCDONOUGH is director of Organizing for Girls for Gender Equity in New York City.

JOYCE PARKER is the founder and director of Citizens for a Better Greenville in Greenville, Mississippi. She is also a member of the Mississippi Delta Catalyst Roundtable and a national leader in the Dignity in Schools Campaign.

CHRISTINA POWELL is a youth leader in the Sisters in Strength program at Girls for Gender Equity in New York City.

CARLOS ROJAS is an organizer and special projects consultant for Youth on Board in Boston, Massachusetts.

ZAKIYA SANKARA-JABAR is cofounder and former executive director of Racial Justice NOW! in Dayton, Ohio. She is the national field organizer for the Dignity in Schools Campaign.

JANNA SHADDUCK-HERNÁNDEZ is a project director at the UCLA Center for Labor Research and Education in Los Angeles. She is also a member of the board of directors of the Building Skills Partnership.

JONATHAN STITH is national director of the Alliance for Educational Justice. He is the father of three young people who went to public schools in Washington, DC.

ROBERTA UDOH is a pre-kindergarten teacher at Young Achievers Science and Math Pilot School, a Boston public school. She is an activist in the Boston Teachers Union and the Boston Educational Justice Alliance.

MARK R. WARREN is professor of public policy and public affairs at the University of Massachusetts Boston. He is a founder and national cochair of the Urban Research-Based Action Network.

VAJRA WATSON is the director of Research and Policy for Equity at the University of California, Davis, and the founder of Sacramento Area Youth Speaks (SAYS).

GEOFFREY WINDER is co-executive director of the Genders and Sexualities Alliance Network, based in Oakland, California.

GLORYA WORNUM is an organizer and former youth leader with Youth on Board in Boston, Massachusetts.

ACKNOWLEDGMENTS

– Mark R. Warren –

FIRST OF ALL, I would like to thank all of the contributors to this book and the other movement builders who participated in the convenings around the book for their dedication and their leadership in the cause of educational justice. I would also like to thank the many other organizers, parent and youth leaders, and education activists who are working hard to build a new future for our young people. I have learned so much from these movement builders and I am constantly inspired by their love and commitment to young people. I am humbled to be partners with them in the struggle for social justice and honored to help them tell their stories and share their wisdom in this book and elsewhere.

I would also like to thank my friends and colleagues in the Urban Research-Based Action Network (URBAN) for their support in our collective effort to create participatory and collaborative forms of knowledge production that help build movements for racial and social justice. I have learned so much from these amazing activist scholars, including José Calderón, Michelle Fine, Dayna Cunningham, Celina Su, John Diamond, Ron Glass, Tim Eatman, Michael Johnson, Julio Cammarota, Sean Ginwright, Joyce King, and so many others. Jeannie Oakes, Bill Ayers, John Rogers, Sara Lawrence-Lightfoot, Karen Mapp, Kavitha Mediratta, Lori Bezahler, and many other friends and colleagues also offered terrific advice and important support for me and this book along the way.

We write this book in troubling times. I would like to thank my friends and colleagues in both these spaces—the educational justice network and URBAN—for creating a community where people care about and support each other and for making movement building joyful and nurturing to our souls. In this spirit, I would like to offer special appreciation to Najma Na-zy'at whose love for young people and passion for organizing and social justice lift me—and so many others—up.

I give warm thanks to the Dignity in Schools Campaign and designer Brian Butter for allowing us to use the campaign's Lift Us Up, Don't Push Us Out! slogan and graphic for the title and cover of this book.

I would like to thank the Ford Foundation, NEA Foundation, and Nellie Mae Education Foundation for financial support for the book project and to hold the meetings that brought the contributors together. Sanjiv Rao and Claribel Vidal were thought partners at the Ford Foundation; they helped shape the project and encouraged others to participate.

I would also like to thank Lindsay Morgia and Jeffrey Moyer, doctoral students at UMass Boston, who provided assistance with organizing the meetings and preparing the book. Jeff's enthusiasm for this project, his genuine care for everyone involved, his close attention to detail, and his amazing skill at IT and social media applications provided invaluable support. We could not have done this without him.

Many people at UMass Boston helped make the meetings and book a success. I would like to thank Andrew King, Andrea Ward, Rashelle Brown, Lisa Greggo, James Stark, Michael Gaughan, Robert O'Keefe, Christopher Brindley, and all the other staff who provided assistance in various ways. David Cash, the dean of the McCormack Graduate School, and Christine Brenner, the chairperson of the Department of Public Policy and Public Affairs, were enthusiastic about this project and offered support all along the way.

I would also like to thank Rachael Marks and the wonderful folks at Beacon Press. They embraced our vision of this book as a tool for movement building and have offered helpful suggestions and professional assistance to make it a reality.

In the end, I would like to thank my family for their inspiration and support. My late father, Russell Warren, taught me the values of labor organizing and racial justice as a child. He believed in a future of freedom and justice for all the world's people, and that vision has inspired me all my life.

Roberta Udoh is my partner in life, love, and activism. With her passion for children and their families, her absolute intolerance for racism and injustice in any form, and her brilliant mind and creative spirit, she anchors and supports me and brings joy to my life.

Our beautiful daughters, Folasade and Imoh, are always full of encouraging words as they find their own way in the world as amazing young women of color. They inspire me and remind me why we commit our lives to the struggle for educational justice: to create a future where all of our young people can develop as free and creative human beings.

NOTES

INTRODUCTION

1. For a more extensive discussion of the analysis presented in this section and citations for the claims made, see Mark R. Warren, "Transforming Public Education: The Need for an Educational Justice Movement," *New England Journal of Public Policy* 26, no. 1 (2014), article 11, http://scholarworks.umb.edu/nejpp /vol26/iss1/11.

1 "I CAN'T MAKE A TEACHER LOVE MY SON"

1. Learn to Earn Dayton, *Know the Gap, Close the Gap* (Dayton, OH: Learn to Earn Dayton, 2017), 25–27.
2. Jawanza Kunjufu, *Understanding Black Male Learning Styles* (Chicago: African American Images, 2010), 38.
3. Jawanza Kunjufu, *Countering the Conspiracy to Destroy Black Boys*, vol. 1 (Chicago: African American Images, 1983), chapter 2.
4. Racial Justice NOW!, *2014 Ohio School Discipline Report Card* (Dayton, OH: Racial Justice Now, 2016).
5. Ibid.
6. Bruce Western and Becky Pettit, "Incarceration & Social Inequality," *Daedalus* 139, no. 3 (2010): 8–19.
7. Racial Justice NOW!, *2014 Report Card*.

2 #SOUTHLAPARENTLOVE

1. CADRE, *Redefining Dignity in Our Schools* (Los Angeles: CADRE, 2010), 6; CADRE, *How Can You Love the Kids but Hate the Parents?* (Los Angeles: CADRE, 2017), 12.

4 FIGHTING FOR GENDER JUSTICE

1. "The Schools Girls Deserve," Girls for Gender Equity, http://www.ggenyc.org /the-schools-girls-deserve, accessed December 8, 2017.

5 THE FREEDOM TO LEARN

1. Padres & Jóvenes Unidos, *The North High School Report: The Voice of Over 700 Students* (Denver: Padres & Jóvenes Unidos, 2004).
2. Padres & Jóvenes Unidos and Advancement Project, *Lessons in Racial Justice & Movement Building: Dismantling the School to Prison Pipeline in Colorado and Nationally* (Denver: Padres & Jóvenes Unidos, 2014), 32.

6 #FIGHTFORDYETT

1. Curtis Black, "Grassroots Success at Dyett High," *Chicago Newstips*, December 2, 2008, http://www.newstips.org/2008/12/grassroots-success-at-dyett-high, accessed January 8, 2018; Sarah Karp, "A Second Chance: Mentoring, Better Discipline Steers Dyett Teens Away from Trouble," *Chicago Reporter*, December 5, 2008, http://www.chicagoreporter.com/second-chance-mentoring-better -discipline-steers-dyett-teens-away-trouble, accessed January 8, 2018.
2. "Tweets per Day: #Fightfordyett and #Wesupportdyett15, August 16th–September 15th," Topsy, accessed September 16, 2015 from Topsy.com.

8 THE SCHOOL IS THE HEART OF THE COMMUNITY

1. Motoko Rich, "Where Are the Teachers of Color?," *New York Times*, April 11, 2015.

9 FIGHTING FOR TEACHERS, CHILDREN, AND THEIR PARENTS

1. "CPS Stats and Facts," Chicago Public Schools website, https://cps.edu/About _CPS/At-a-glance/Pages/Stats_and_facts.aspx, last modified November 13, 2017.

10 #ENDWARONYOUTH

1. Daniel Losen et al., *Are We Closing the School Discipline Gap?* (Los Angeles: Center for Civil Rights Remedies, 2015).
2. Audre Lorde, "Learning from the 60s," in *Sister Outsider: Essays and Speeches by Audre Lorde*, rev. ed. (New York: Crossing Press, 2007), 138.
3. Evie Blad, "United Nations Panel Recommends Changes to U.S. School Discipline," *Rules for Engagement* (blog), *Education Week*, February 1, 2016, http:// blogs.edweek.org/edweek/rulesforengagement/2016/02/united_nations_panel _recommends_changes_to_us_school_discipline.html.

11 TEACHERS UNITE!

1. Audre Lorde, "A Burst of Light: Living with Cancer," in *I Am Your Sister: Collected and Unpublished Writings of Audre Lorde*, ed. Rudolph P. Byrd, Johnnetta Betsch Cole, and Beverly Guy-Sheftal (New York: Oxford University Press, 2009), 140.
2. Elizabeth Sullivan and Elizabeth Keeney, *Teachers Talk: School Culture, Safety, and Human Rights* (New York: NESRI and Teachers Unite, 2008), 33.
3. Eve L. Ewing, "Chicago Responds to President Trump: Artists, Writers, Musicians, Academics, Activists, and Politicians—Even Rahm!—Weigh In on the New Administration: The Threats, the Fears, the Absurdity," *Chicago Reader*, January 19, 2017, https://www.chicagoreader.com/chicago/donald-trump -president-inauguration-responses/Content?oid=25132990.

13 SYSTEM CHANGE

1. Los Angeles Unified School District (LAUSD), "Latino Heritage Month," n.d., https://home.lausd.net/apps/news/article/400975; LAUSD, "Food That's In, When School Is Out," June 7, 2013, https://home.lausd.net/apps/news/article/314909.
2. Hillel Aron, "The Number of Children in L.A. Is Shrinking—Which Could Be a Disaster," *LA Weekly*, March 2, 2017, http://www.laweekly.com/news/the -number-of-children-in-la-is-shrinking-which-could-be-a-disaster-7986526.

3. LAUSD, "Suspensions Down—Student Safety Up," August 17, 2012, https://home.lausd.net/apps/news/article/262220.

4. LAUSD, "School Discipline Data Reports—Suspension, 2016–2017 School Year," http://schoolinfosheet.lausd.net.

5. Mitchell Landsberg, "L.A. Sees Graduation Rates Drop," *Los Angeles Times*, June 21, 2008, http://articles.latimes.com/2008/jun/21/local/me-grads21; Mike Szymanski, "LAUSD's Graduation Rate Tops 80 Percent, Surpassing Its Own Goals," *LA School Report*, September 12, 2017, http://laschoolreport.com/lausds-graduation-rate-tops-80-percent-surpassing-its-own-goals.

15 #SCHOOLISMYHUSTLE

1. Steve Biko, "Black Consciousness and the Quest for a True Humanity," *Ufahamu: A Journal of African Studies* 8, no. 3 (1978): 6.

2. US Census Bureau, *American Community Survey 1-Year Estimates* (2016), retrieved from *Census Reporter* profile page for California, https://censusreporter.org/profiles/04000US06-california.

3. Leigh Patel, *Decolonizing Educational Research: From Ownership to Answerability* (London: Routledge, 2016), 4.

4. Paulo Freire, *Pedagogy of the Oppressed* (New York: Herder and Herder, 1970), 69.

16 JANITORS ARE PARENTS TOO!

1. Veronica Terriquez, "Schools for Democracy: Labor Union Participation and the School-Based Civic Engagement of Latino Immigrant Parents," *American Sociological Review* 76, no. 4 (2011): 581–601.

17 THE SAME STRUGGLE

1. US Bureau of the Census, Statistical Abstract (Washington, DC: US Government Printing Office, 2015).

2. Ibid.

3. José Calderón and Pomona Habla Coalition, unpublished research (2008).

4. Ernesto Arce, "Pomona Residents March Against Racist Checkpoints," *Liberation*, June 3, 2008, 1.

5. Calderón and Pomona Habla Coalition, unpublished research.

ABOUT THE AUTHORS

MARK R. WARREN is professor of public policy and public affairs at the University of Massachusetts, Boston, and a founder and cochair of the Urban Research-Based Action Network. His previous books include *Dry Bones Rattling: Community Building to Revitalize American Democracy*, *Fire in the Heart: How White Activists Embrace Racial Justice*, and *A Match on Dry Grass: Community Organizing as a Catalyst for School Reform*. A John Simon Guggenheim Memorial Fellow, Warren studies and works with community and youth organizing groups seeking to promote equity and justice in education, community development, and American democratic life.

DAVID GOODMAN is an award-winning independent journalist and author of numerous books, including four *New York Times* best sellers coauthored with his sister, *Democracy Now!* host Amy Goodman. Goodman's articles have also appeared in *Mother Jones*, the *Washington Post*, *Los Angeles Times*, *Christian Science Monitor*, *Boston Globe*, *Nation*, *Outside*, and other publications. He has been a frequent guest on national radio and television shows and networks including PBS *NewsHour*, *Democracy Now!*, NPR's *Fresh Air*, *Morning Edition*, C-SPAN, and CNN.